CAUGHT
IN THE FRAME

A student of the game, Barbados. Photograph: Gordon Brooks

CAUGHT IN THE FRAME

150 YEARS OF CRICKET PHOTOGRAPHY

PATRICK EAGAR

Main text by Nick Yapp
Picture research by Richard Wilson

Published in association with

National Power

CollinsWillow
An Imprint of HarperCollins*Publishers*

First published in 1992 by
Collins Willow
an imprint of HarperCollins Publishers
London

© Patrick Eagar and Richard Wilson 1992

A CIP catalogue record for this book
is available from the British Library

ISBN 0 00 218393 5

Edited and designed by
Toucan Books Limited
Albion Courtyard
Greenhills Rents
London EC1M 6BN

Printed and bound in Spain by Graficromo

Contents

Acknowledgements

The authors and publishers would like to thank the following photographers, agencies and organisations who have provided photographs for *Caught in the Frame*:

The George Beldam Collection; Mrs Pam Roberts, Curator, The Royal Photographic Society, Bath; Tim McCann, Assistant Archivist, West Sussex Records Office; G. Wilson, Secretary, Priory Park Cricket Club; The Roger Mann Collection; Stephen Green, Curator, Marylebone Cricket Club; Edwin Wallace, Victoria & Albert Museum Picture Library; Dawn Wyman, The Hulton Picture Company; Brendan Quinlan, Aerofilms; The John Whybrow Collection; Alasdair Hawkyard, Harrow School Archivist, The Governors of Harrow School; Paul Kurton, Sport & General; Mrs A. Hadfield, Press Association; Patrick Eagar; Ken Kelly; Graham Morris; David Munden, *The Cricketer;* Adrian Murrell, All-Sport; Dennis Oulds; Ken Saunders. In addition David Frith has been most helpful with advice, and his book *Pageant of Cricket* has been invaluable.

Foreword

The sight of a Walter Hammond or a Donald Bradman driving through the covers was poetry in motion. With acute eye and immaculate timing, they had the intuitive cricketers' gifts, passed down from illustrious predecessors and, thankfully, passed on to today's cricketing heroes.

Capturing this motion and 'freezing' it on celluloid is another art form, and here is another memorable record of talented men behind the camera lens preserving for posterity great performances with bat and ball.

This timely volume will bring back memories for the cricket enthusiast and will delight aficianados of the camera's eye.

JOHN BAKER
Chief Executive
National Power plc

Introduction
by Patrick Eagar

SOME TIME around 1826 the Frenchman M. Nicéphore Niépce spent eight hours taking a photograph of the courtyard outside his attic window. After years of experimenting, he finally succeeded in producing a permanent photograph of the view from his window in Gras, near Chalon-sur-Saône. It was at least nine years before anyone else came up with something that could be regarded as a photograph.

Second in the race to produce a photograph was an Englishman – William Henry Fox Talbot – who succeeded in making a paper negative of the lattice window of his library at Lacock Abbey in 1837, some five years after Thomas Lord died. His process was much closer to what would eventually become the standard conventional photography process we know today. However, he too had to wait for his images, half-an-hour being an average exposure time. The advantage of his process was that having made a negative, the same process could be repeated on it to make any number of identical paper positive prints.

The first commercially successful photographic process was invented by a Frenchman – Louis Daguerre. He published details of his discovery in 1839 and in 1841 the first public studio in Europe was opened in London. For twenty years or more the daguerreotype, as it was known, was the photographic medium of professional photographers. It was still not the instantaneous process we are used to today; exposures generally being measured in minutes rather than fractions of a second. Nevertheless the first photograph of a cricketer was probably taken on a daguerreotype.

W.G. Grace was not born until 1848, by which time commercial daguerreotype studios were widespread. Various other photographic processes were invented and developed; each searching for greater convenience for the photographer and enhanced film speed – essential for instantaneous exposures.

Roger Fenton took his camera to the

The captains of England
and Australia during the
1924-25 Test series in
Australia –
A.E.R. Gilligan and
H.L. Collins. Both
captains appear conscious
of the camera, but the pipe
is a joy.
Photograph: Herbert
Fishwick

Crimean War in 1855. He was successful in his mission and was able to take 300 or so photographs of the troops although, with minimum exposures of three seconds, none was an action photograph. Fenton has a significance in the history of cricket photography too; perhaps the earliest photograph showing a cricket match was taken by him in 1857.

There are many general scenes of cricket matches dating from the 1860s; but careful examination will show that they are all taken at moments of minimum action – a bowler at the end of his run, or a pause while the captain was setting his field.

The first photographer to make a systematic study of athletes and animals in action was the English-born Eadweard Muybridge; his action sequences froze the motion of people jumping, running, wrestling and somersaulting. He even photographed sequences of a cricketer while preparing his book, *Animal Locomotion,* which was published in 1887. He used exposures as short as a two-thousandths of a second.

At about this time, general views of cricket matches tended to be taken at more adventurous moments. The frozen flight of the moving ball can frequently be spotted in photographs of the 1880s. In 1889 *Wisden Cricketers' Almanack* included photographs for the first time. These consisted of original photographic portraits which were pasted into each copy. They were taken by 'the well known Brighton firm of E. Hawkins and Co'.

One of the earliest photographers to make a systematic effort to photograph first-class cricketers was E. Hawkins of Brighton. He, or perhaps more accurately the firm, seldom

Cricket on the Sixth-Form Ground, Harrow School, late nineteenth century.
Source: Harrow School Archives

attempted to freeze the action, and the photographs still widely seen in books and along pavilion walls are really very static. Hawkins advertised in the 1889 edition and referred to a photograph of the Australians in the field – 'a splendid photograph - taken in one twentieth part of a second'. If this was Hawkins's available shutter speed it would explain the lack of dynamic action in the exceptionally sharp photographs.

By 1899 W.A. Rouch and other contributors to *The Graphic* were taking photographs at high shutter speeds and the age of the live 'action' photograph had arrived.

George Beldam, Middlesex amateur (1900-1907) and scratch golfer, was a pioneer sports photographer. His cricket work remains largely intact thanks to the diligence of his son, also named George Beldam, who looks after it. Most people would immediately recognise several of his images, especially the classic one of Victor Trumper stepping out to drive. His shutter-speeds of up to one-thousandth of a second were in contrast to the one-twentieth of a second mentioned by Hawkins & Co. some fifteen years earlier. Beldam clearly enjoyed pushing the existing technology to its limits. He describes the use of an electric release developed for bird and animal photography, which enabled the photographer to take photographs using a 25-yard cord. He used it so that he could bowl to his subjects (right-handed) and take the photograph with his left hand, thus being able to anticipate the stroke that the batsman might make. He was also able to save plates that would have otherwise have been wasted, since he knew immediately if the wrong ball had been bowled for a given stroke.

Beldam also took his camera to Test matches, and although he was able to use shutter speeds that would be capable of freezing any action, he was not able to capture the action close to the boundary. It seems that Beldam would have had sufficient introduction to grounds such as Lord's, the Oval and Trent Bridge to be allowed to set up his camera in positions of his own choosing.

In later years, as the number of photographers increased, the siting of them in reasonable positions was to become more of a problem. Nevertheless there is a spot at Lord's that appears to have been the exclusive territory of the stills cricket photographer for over 100 years and remains so to this day. It is immediately underneath the new electronic scoreboard adjacent to the Tavern Stand.

In the years leading up to the First World War, more photographs were published in newspapers and magazines. The first use of a really long lens appears to be around 1909.

An advertisement in Wisden's Cricketers' Almanack for 1899. 'Batting and bowling positions' would still be almost entirely posed.

From then photographers had the equipment to record action close to the boundary.

The First World War led to the development of photo-reconnaissance from specially adapted aircraft. In order to be safe from anti-aircraft fire the planes would fly at a minimum height of 5000 feet and frequently much higher. There was a demand for newer, better and longer lenses. They needed to be at least 20 inches (500mm) in focal length and the longer ones were 28 inches (700mm) or more. By 1920 a number of different English Ross and German Zeiss lenses were available, of suitable lengths for cricket.

Any of these lenses could be specially adapted to fit reflex plate cameras of the day – mostly half-plate (4³/4 in x 6¹/2 in). Many used the Shew reflex. With little modification these were to remain the standard cricket cameras for an astonishing fifty years. Although the standard press plate was already 5in x 4in or 12cm x 9cm, the extra image area provided by the half plate was important for cricket. A print from the whole of the negative would include a number of fielders beside the batsman – obviously crucial for catches by the slips and other close fielders. Much of this extra detail was to be superfluous; the problem with photographing cricket is, and always has been, that it is quite impossible to anticipate where the action will occur next. The image on the plate would, however, be big enough to enlarge small details. The batsman would be the most likely subject, but there would always be the option of concentrating on some other detail – say a spectacular catch in the slips cordon.

Soon after the War, the English Test grounds licensed the rights for stills photography to a single agency – they did the same thing with the movie rights, selling exclusive rights to a single newsreel company. The Sport & General agency handled stills at Lord's and Central Press Photos handled stills at the Oval. The remaining four Test match grounds were split between them. Sport & General usually covered Test matches at Headingley and Central Press those at Old

Trafford, Trent Bridge and Edgbaston. The local papers in each area were allowed access to Test matches, but the photographs they took were only for their own use. This situation continued right up to the end of 1971.

The system led to many farcical interludes. Not to be outdone, a large number of the excluded stills and movie cameramen would set up outside the ground. They would rent space in flats overlooking the action, or would build scaffolding towers. In reply, the official agencies would take careful stock of the situation. Before play started on the first day was a time

D.G. (Sir Donald) Bradman practising in the nets at Lord's, 1948. It was rare for agencies to use colour at that time.
Source: Sport & General

for reconnaissance and planning. They would check on the angles of the maverick emplacements from the middle of the field and decide which of a number of possible counter-measures was required.

Their armoury was extensive. They would use a large mirror to reflect the sun's rays into the lenses of the rival news teams. If there was no sun, or the angles were wrong, they would use netting and bunting. A few rows of small flags which could be raised or lowered simply and quickly was an effective deterrent and would have been of equal use against stills and movies. At Trent Bridge one year, they even used a small barrage balloon – again easily raised and lowered to thwart the pirates. This, unfortunately, was subject to counter-attack and in the lunch interval one of the excluded rivals paid for admission at the gate. He then chopped the balloon free of its moorings with a pocket knife.

No such restrictions applied in Australia, and

the first photographer to take advantage of the new post-war technology was Herbert Fishwick. He had migrated from England in his twenties and built an enviable reputation as the principal photographer of the *Sydney Mail* as well as the *Sydney Morning Herald*. Over the years he was responsible for most of the memorable cricket images taken in Australia. The classic photograph of Hammond's cover drive comes immediately to mind.

Throughout the inter-war period the half-plate camera remained the only serious piece of equipment for cricket photography. At that time Central Press Photos would use three photographers for major matches, with a fourth roaming the ground with a smaller camera for off-the-cuff shots of spectators, and for general views of a crowded ground – anything that might appeal to picture editors. For years the senior man was George Frankland and he would operate a 48-inch lens on the first floor balcony of the Oval pavilion, adjacent to what

P.F. Warner (Sir Pelham 1873-1963) manager of the MCC Touring Team to Australia 1932-1933 meets the staff commander of the SS Orontes *prior to their departure to Australia.*
Left to right:
G.O. Allen, L.E.G. Ames, F.R. Brown, Master of SS Orontes, *P.F. Warner, W.E. Bowes, D.R. Jardine, W.R. Hammond, H. Larwood, M. Leyland, T.B. Mitchell, E. Paynter, H. Sutcliffe, H. Verity. The creases in the trousers suggest a photo-session was expected.*

is now the Committee Room. His main responsibility would be for batting photographs, and catches in the arc from wicketkeeper to third slip, and possibly short leg. A second, Jimmy Sime, would be posted on the top floor of the pavilion, pointing a 30-inch lens down the wicket – with his wider lens he would have been looking for any catches from gully to short leg, at both ends. The third man, Walter Lockyear, was stationed on the roof of the Vauxhall stand. Using another 48-inch lens he would get the benefit of the late afternoon Oval sun and would take the exact opposite view to Frankland – thus increasing the chances of obtaining a good photograph of any incident.

In 1934 Dennis Oulds appeared at his first Test match as a messenger boy for Central Press Photos. He was to photograph cricket professionally for the next fifty years. He remembers covering the Oval Test in 1946 from a flat outside the ground. This could be a comparatively comfortable way of spending a week, especially if one had a sympathetic

landlady who would supply cups of tea at the right moments. Oulds had a multitude of memorable photographs, but his personal favourite is the one of all eleven England players crowding Graeme McKenzie at the Oval in 1968. Only the square leg umpire was missing from the photograph.

Sport & General continued at Lord's in a similar way up to 1973. Vic Fowler, Brian Thomas and Ken Saunders were the last from Sport & General to use the Long Tom.

In Australia Harry Martin became the cricket specialist of the *Sydney Morning Herald*, covering every big game from November 1946 onwards. He shared the honours with Ron Lovitt of *The Age* at the tied Test at Brisbane in 1960. They were the only two photographers present during the closing overs and were both working with plate cameras. They realised there was quite a good chance of neither of them getting the crucial photograph unless they agreed to cooperate. From analysis of the photographs published in Jack Fingleton's *The Greatest Test of All* it seems that for the final

An assortment of press cameras to photograph the touring West Indians at the Duke of Norfolk's ground, Arundel Castle in 1969.
Photograph: Patrick Eagar

over at least Martin would take the stroke, whatever happened – Lovitt would take whatever followed. One can imagine Martin frantically reloading as Lovitt coolly waited for Solomon's throw to hit the stumps for that most memorable of cricket photographs.

In 1964-65 Harry Martin became the first cricket specialist to abandon the traditional Long Tom in favour of 35mm. Martin and many others rapidly decided that the many disadvantages of the plate camera were beginning to outweigh the few advantages. The Long Tom had reigned unchallenged for more than forty years, but there were many limitations to its use.

For a start, once a plate camera had been set up for the day, it was not easy to move it or change its position. An incident on the boundary would seldom have been recorded before the advent of 35mm, since there was no way of aiming and refocusing the big camera in a hurry. It was hard enough repositioning the camera every six balls. Once a photograph had been taken it would be at least five seconds

before the camera was ready to take another.

Roll film, and especially 35mm cameras, suffered from none of these disadvantages. Winding on film by hand was infinitely faster than the changing of a dark slide (sheet film holder) and the subsequent manual cocking of the shutter. The advent of motor drives in the late 1960s would allow two or three frames per second and eventually as many as six.

While Sport & General, Central Press and many other agencies continued to use Long Toms in England, the Australians and various individuals in England, including Ken Kelly and myself, appreciated the advantages of 35mm. Kelly, who had been photographing Test matches for local papers in Leeds and Birmingham since 1938, had worked out a cunning system of using more than one camera at a time – using one lens, a 600mm for close-ups and one or sometimes two others for the wider views. This to a large extent equalised the one remaining advantage that the Long Tom had over 35mm. You could photograph a batsman or bowler close-up and still be

prepared for the catch at second slip.

By now the authorities in England had relented and the exclusive arrangement with the agencies came to an end. In 1972 the doors were thrown open to Fleet Street newspapers and specialist cricket photographers.

Colour film now began to be used regularly. Newspapers were able to choose their own angles and techniques. On the whole the agencies had been conservative in their choice of angles but it has to be noted that they hardly missed an incident and it is a tribute to the many photographers who worked with the large cameras over the years that so much was photographed – more, I suspect, than is generally the case today. In the age of the personality cult, when Ian Botham's mere presence at a match guarantees a front page picture of him in many papers, an otherwise excellent photograph of a wicket falling is likely as not to find its way into the bin.

As technology continued to develop new cameras, lenses, films and accessories, the imaginative photographer could adapt these to his own techniques. Expanding on Kelly's concept of using two or more cameras at the same spot, subsequently it became possible to control a second or third camera at any distance using a radio or infra-red link. Thus it was possible to set up cameras at any point in the ground and control them from a single spot. Furthermore, state-of-the art lenses and high-speed films provided entirely adequate images.

Today many 35mm cameras are electronically controlled to be auto-exposure and auto-focus. Motor drives can fire at twelve frames per second. Allied with the very high-quality lenses and cameras available, the results are technically excellent. However, they are not necessarily any better than those photographs of Victor Trumper in 1908, Walter Hammond in 1928, Don Bradman in 1948 or Gary Sobers in 1968.

The future points firmly to the eventual introduction, when their quality improves, of electronic images – photography without film or the still equivalent of the television picture. Newspapers need photographs in a hurry and while images have been sent along telephone lines for half a century or more, the modern trend to colour photographs will ensure that within five years all newspaper photographs will be taken without the use of film. Over the past few years, the image has to be made on film, which after processing (often at a 'mini-lab' conveniently close to the cricket ground), is scanned – converting it into a form that can be sent by telephone using a portable photo transmitting machine.

The introduction of negative (as opposed to print) transmitters by Nikon in 1984 and more lately of colour transmitters by Nikon, Hasselblad and Leefax has revolutionised the procedure. Graham Morris, Adrian Murrell and others have been sending photographs back to England from hotel rooms and sometimes directly from cricket grounds on winter tours for some time.

Before long, high-quality images will be produced in a digital form by the camera itself and will be instantly available for transmitting down digital phone lines into a digital store in the newspaper's computer. Using telephones linked by a portable satellite dish, this might mean that it will be possible for a photographer to transmit a photograph from anywhere in the world completely independently of any local facilities. No dark room or mini-lab and no telephone exchange will be necessary. The whole process from taking the photograph to arrival on the picture editor's desk would take just a few minutes. The first time that anyone would see it as a print on paper would be as the copies roll off the printing presses.

While it is hoped that they would still recognise the game of cricket, it would seem that Messrs. Hawkins, Rouch and Beldam would have quite a surprise if they could see what has become of their pioneering photographic labours.

The popular pastime of beach cricket being played on Barbados' Accra beach at sunset. One of the players is Gordon Greenidge.
Photograph: Patrick Eagar

CHAPTER 1

The Early Years 1839-65

'If photography is allowed to stand in for art in some of its functions
it will soon supplant or corrupt it completely, thanks to the natural
support it will find in the stupidity of the multitude.'
— Charles Baudelaire, 1859

IN MANY WAYS, the science and art of photography grew alongside the science and art of cricket. Both had their origins further back in history than most perhaps realise. The *camera obscura* was operating during the lifetime of Leonardo da Vinci. There are pictorial representations of a game at least resembling cricket, dating from the fourteenth century, an illustration from *The Romance of Alexander*. There are also paintings, perhaps not authentic, of cricket in Elizabethan times, and certainly a woodcut of cricket in 1720. One of the most frequently reproduced pictures of early cricket is Francis Hayman's painting of *Cricket on the Artillery Ground, Finsbury*, which dates from 1743. In the same year a Frenchman, Louis Boitard, produced *An Exact representation of the Game of Cricket - Inscribed to all gentlemen lovers of that Diversion*. From the middle of the eighteenth century cricket pictures became almost commonplace, whether paintings, watercolours, engravings, or sketches.

Photography, like cricket, began as an age of the gifted amateur, emerging from unsettled times. Lord's itself finally came to rest only in 1812, and the Mitchelson brothers were still growing their vegetables on Kennington Oval twenty years later. Cricket was still a rough and dangerous game played on rough and dangerous ground, where the busiest player was usually behind the wicket. Some fast underarm bowlers required three longstops. Not until 1836 did the Sussex Cricket Club establish a fund to finance the playing of county matches, and the following year William IV generously and graciously donated twenty pounds. The great names in cricket at this time were 'Felix' (Nicholas Wanostracht), Fuller Pilch, Alfred Mynn and William 'Nonpareil' Lillywhite. Top hats were still being worn by fielders, round–arm bowling was a recent innovation (1827), and the wet clay of the art of batting had yet to be moulded by the likes of Grace and Gunn, Shrewsbury and Shaw. The very names of the matches from this era suggest an attractive lack

R. PILLING.

Four carte-de-visite
photographs:
Top left to right: R. Peel
1857-1941 Yorkshire,
J. Briggs 1862-1902
Lancashire.
Bottom left to right:
R. Pilling 1855-1891
Lancashire, W. Oscroft
1843-1905
Nottinghamshire.
Source: Marylebone
Cricket Club

of formal timetabling: Teetotallers v Whiskey Drinkers ('...the patrons of the mountain dew won the match by 35....'), One-Arm Pensioners v One-Leg Pensioners (the One-Arm Pensioners won by 157 runs), Married v Single (a closely fought contest which Single won by three wickets).

Regular reporting of MCC and other important matches began in *The Times* in 1842, the reports coming largely from the dip-pen of William Denison, freelance reporter, keen cricketer, and publisher of Denison's *Cricketers' Companion*, a forerunner of *Wisden*. The only illustrations of cricket were engravings, oil paintings, lithographs and watercolours – prettily composed, but static affairs. Cricket

scenes were also to be found on plates, punch bowls, silk handkerchiefs, fish strainers, and in political cartoons and satirical prints (such as that of the Duke of Dorset and company in the *Rambler's Magazine* of 1784). All these pictures were more in the nature of landscapes with figures than lifelike representations of cricket itself. So it had been since the mid-eighteenth century, so it was to remain during this early period of cricket photography.

For, whatever the brilliance and revolutionary qualities of their new techniques, the pioneers of photography clung to older, existing artistic inspirations. The early images of Nicéphore Niépce, Louis-Jacques Mande Daguerre and William Henry Fox Talbot were captured with equipment that weighed upwards of 150 pounds, and required exposures ranging from several hours to fifteen minutes. A painting might have been quicker in some cases, and it's hardly surprising that all these early photographic reproductions were of 'posed' subjects and owed much to traditional rules of composition. Only a grafter capable of out-stonewalling 'Slasher' Mackay, Mudassar Nazar or Trevor Bailey would have been a suitable cricket subject. Despite this traditional and academic approach, early photography came in for much criticism. A panel of competition judges at the Great Exhibition in 1851 declared that: 'Unfortunately, in this industry, good taste cannot always be said to reign supreme.' Fifty years later, when the science had made great technical progress, George Beldam and C.B. Fry, who published their highly successful *Great Batsmen, Their Methods at a Glance* in 1905, were faced with the same problem of taste. 'It has been said,' wrote Fry, 'that the results of instantaneous photography, however true to nature, are generally inartistic in effect: "very true but very ugly".'

Although there is a portrait from 1851 of William Lambert, the outstanding all-rounder who scored a century in each innings for Sussex v Epsom at Lord's in 1817, the earliest cricket photograph that we have is almost certainly that taken by Roger Fenton on 25 July 1857 of the field of play for the match between the Royal Artillery and Hunsdonbury. From 1853 to 1856, Fenton had toured the Crimea with his 'Photographic Carriage', taking pictures of French, British and Turkish soldiers in camp, the Valley of Death along which the Light Brigade had so heroically charged, and the aftermath of the siege of Sebastopol.

Fenton used the newly invented wet collodion process. This consisted of first coating a glass plate with an emulsion, running from the darkroom van, inserting the holder in the camera, making the exposure which lasted anywhere from three to twenty seconds, and rushing back to process the glass plate negative before the emulsion could dry. Heat, dust, high winds, even the breath of the photographer could ruin the plates. The whole operation took between five and eight minutes. One of the problems with the wet collodion process was that it could not be used on very hot days, making it hardly suitable for the summer season. Fenton complained: 'The heat sends the stoppers flying out of my bottles and spoils every picture'.

Nevertheless, the Hunsdonbury photograph, which is one of a series of four pictures that Fenton took, is a triumph. It is posed, but realistically so. Most of the fielders are crouching, prepared for the next delivery - the practice of walking in as the bowler bowled was seldom seen until Murdoch's Australians used it so devastatingly in support of Spofforth and Boyle at the Oval in the Ashes Test of 1882. There is much detail to be enjoyed in Fenton's picture: the little tent for the scorers, the ladies in their crinolines, the telegraph board, the top hatted umpire, the two gentlemen sitting on a bench under the trees. Nevertheless, it is still a landscape rather than a sports picture. Strangely, Fenton abandoned photography in 1862.

The only other categories of early cricket photographs that we have are the portrait and the group picture. In portraits, the subjects looked straight to camera, often in mufti but holding some piece of cricket impedimenta as evidence of their trade or calling – in the same way that the gamekeepers and fishermen held gun or rod for Fox Talbot or Hill and Adamson. David Octavius Hill and Robert Adamson were the two greatest exponents of the process known as 'calotype' (literally – 'beautiful picture'). Their technical and artistic partnership lasted only five years, from 1843 to 1848, by which time Fox Talbot's negative/positive system had begun to supercede all others.

By the time these first photographs were taken, the giants of the late eighteenth and early nineteenth century game were all long

An early location shot. The first overseas touring team managed by Fred Lillywhite sailed from Liverpool to North America on 7 September 1859. Back row, left to right: R.P. Carpenter, W. Caffyn, T. Lockyer, H.H. Stephenson (crouching), G. Parr (capt), J. Grundy, J. Caesar, T. Hayward Seated: J. Wisden (left), J. Jackson (right) Front, left to right: A.J.D. Diver, John Lillywhite Source: The Royal Photgraphic Society, Bath

retired. Sadly, we have no photograph of Thomas Lord, though we do have paintings and silhouettes of him. There are, however, fine portraits of Edward Budd, Fuller Pilch, Mrs Martha Grace (W.G.'s mother), and there exists one of John Wisden of Sussex holding a ball in his hand, and another of William Beldham in old age with both hands firmly planted round the handle of a bat. This was taken in 1857, the same year as Fenton's

photograph, when Beldham was ninety-one years old. 'Silver Billy' Beldham has been reckoned by some the Bradman of his age. His 144 for MCC against Middlesex in 1792 was the highest ever score at Old Lord's. Beldham was ninety-six when he died in 1862, and this photograph is the only one we have of a cricketer who played at Hambledon before that illustrious club was dissolved in 1791 and its fine players were scattered the length and

Sussex County Cricket Club. Left to right (standing): G.W. King, J.H. Hale, C. Smith, G.F. Salter, B. Stent (secretary), H. Stubberfield, C. Ellis, C. Payne, R. Fillery, J. Dean (Umpire). Left to right (seated): C. Horwood, James Lillywhite (Jun), G. Wells, John Lillywhite Source: West Sussex Record Office (MS 2360)/Priory Park Cricket Club

breadth of England. Beldham, who had a reputation for being a great gossip as well as a great cricketer, also played in the very first season at the original site of Lord's. In June 1787, he played for All England against White Conduit Club, scored fifty and was, according to *The Times*, 'by far the best player on the ground'. The best we can do for an action picture of Beldham in his youth, is the watercolour sketch by George Shepheard Snr of around 1790.

Team photographs were perhaps the most original category in pictorial terms. Any group picture is by its very nature posed and artificial, but the photographs of George Parr's England touring party to North America in 1859 have a freshness and a casualness about them that are lacking from the logo-encrusted, militarily drilled equivalents of today. There are several

of the 1859 team, some taken in photographic studios, some on board the *Nova Scotia* in which they sailed to Quebec, taking two weeks to make the Atlantic crossing. In all of the pictures there is a fine sense of 'spread yourselves out, fellows – relax, be natural'. Not everyone looks at the camera, but the quality of the photographs is good enough for all members of the party to be identified and recognised, from the heavily whiskered Parr and Wisden to the stocky Julius Caesar, and the long-legged Diver and William Caffyn. Caffyn was the only player to go on all three of the first tours, to North America in 1859 and to Australia in 1861-62 and 1863-64. He appears in photographs of all three touring parties, sober and dignified, a far cry from the youngster who had had to borrow half a crown to get to his first professional match at the Oval

The year of 'Great Expectations'. The first English team to tour Australia 1861-62. Left to right: W. Mortlock, W. Mudie, G. Bennett, C. Lawrence, H.H. Stephenson (capt), W.B. Hallam (Spiers & Pond Agent), W. Caffyn, G. Griffith, T. Hearne, R. Iddison, T. Sewell (Jun), E. Stepenson. Missing from the group is G. Wells. Source: Marylebone Cricket Club

24

MR W.B. MALLAM.

MORTLOCK. MUDIE. BENNETT. LAWRENCE. H.H.STEPHENSON. CAFFYN. GRIFFITH. HEARNE. IDDISON. SEWELL. E. STEPHENSON.

THE ENGLAND ELEVEN.

Taken just previous to their departure for Australia Oct.r 1861

WITH MR W.B. MALLAM THE AUSTRALIAN REPRESENTATIVE.

London. Published by John Wisden 2 Coventry St. Leicester Square & John Lillywhite Seymour St. Euston Square, and F. Lillywhite Kennington Oval.

in 1848. Sadly, we have no photographs of Caffyn playing the cornet during the voyages, of George Anderson singing, or of Dr E.M. Grace pulling teeth.

One of the best photographs of these early touring groups was that taken of Stephenson's 1859 team by T.H. Hennah on board the *Nova Scotia*. Hennah and Kent were photographic partners who had a licence from Fox Talbot, and who rented premises in the King's Road, Brighton from 1852-73. These premises were known as William Henry Mason's Repository

All England XI (v XXII of Northern Ireland), Belfast, 6-7 September 1860. Photograph by J. Lawrence, Dublin. A stereoscopic pair of photographs. Source: The Roger Mann Collection

of Arts. Mason himself was a dealer in prints, but Brighton rapidly became an important photographic centre. The Hennah and Kent collection of photographs was subsequently taken over by another famous cricket photographer, Charles Hawkins, who continued in the photographic business until 1901. Tragically, the Hennah and Kent collection was destroyed with many of Hawkins's own negatives in 1893 when the King's Road premises were demolished to make way for an extension to the Hotel Metropole.

Other early group photographs included that of the Free Foresters in 1859, the Household Brigade XI at Lord's in 1863, the Sussex team of 1860, I Zingari in 1866, the five Grace Brothers in a West Gloucestershire eleven of 1866, Harrow School Second Team of 1869, and the English team that sailed to Melbourne in the *Great Britain* for a tour of Australia

during the winter of 1861-62, a tour commercially sponsored by Spiers and Pond, restaurant contractors. Quality in these pictures varies enormously. The Household Brigade picture is fine, but that of Stephenson's touring party is poor. The cricketers are packed tightly together in an awkward bundle, with the back row almost totally obscured, save for the manager and agent of Spiers and Pond, Mr Mallam, who presents a splendid John Wilkes Booth figure. Two years later, a far better picture was taken of Parr's 1863-64 touring party, taken at Lord's in the autumn before they sailed. The picture of the Harrow School Second Team suggests that photographers 'liked whate'er they looked on', and were not concerned only with the greatest and most famous.

As we shall see later, it's a mistake to take too parochial a view of the development of cricket photography. Just as photography itself was pioneered separately by different people in different places (Niépce in France, Fox Talbot in England, Hercule Florence in Brazil), so there are photographs of cricket in the mid-nineteenth century taken wherever the game was played: Australia, Kohat (now a part of Pakistan), the Annandale Sports ground in Simla, Hong Kong, North America, South Africa, Japan (the residents team at Yokohama), and even France, where an English Civil Service team played in 1865. There is a picture in the La Trobe Library (Melbourne) of an inter-state match between Victoria and New South Wales taken at Melbourne in 1860. Like Fenton's study at Hunsdonbury three years earlier, this is a posed picture which required the co-operation of players and spectators alike, all of whom had to sit or stand in a state of suspended animation for some time. Like rain and bad light, the photographer had the ability to halt play. Among the excellent photographs taken in Melbourne by C. Nettleton of Stephenson's touring party of 1861-62, there is one of a game in progress when the XVIII of Victoria played the English visitors. Unfortunately, it is all too apparent that the match has come to a grinding halt while the picture is taken, since both square leg and the square leg umpire have turned to look straight to camera.

Once the art and process of photography had become established, there followed what amounted to a photographic mania. Daguerreotypes were enormously popular, one report suggests that over 400,000 were produced in one year in the state of Massachusetts alone. Fox Talbot spent a small fortune on his invention (around £5000, at a time when the average weekly wage fluctuated between £1 and 35p), and recovered scarce one half of that. The London Stereoscopic Company, founded in 1854 by George Swann Nottage, became an immediate success. The double-image slides that it produced were taken with a short exposure and achieved high definition. Both slides and Brewster Stereoscopes were mass produced, and they

were sold cheaply and in vast numbers. By 1856, half a million stereoscopes had been sold, and by 1858 the Company's catalogue contained over 100,000 titles. The firm had their own team of photographers but also bought in the work of others. These pictures were very much for home consumption and enjoyment; newspapers and magazines were not yet ready to print photographic illustrations.

Nevertheless, photography was becoming more and more commercial. At first, photographs were expensive items, but in 1858 the much less expensive *cartes-de-visite* were introduced. These were small pictures, pasted on card, taken from a negative that was divided into six or more images, the area to be exposed changing each time the shutter was opened. Each image measured roughly 4 x 2$^{1}/_{2}$ inches. Many more people could afford these new photographs, for, whereas the normal studio portrait in Paris in 1862 cost anything from twenty-five to a hundred francs, the *cartes-de-visite* cost fifteen francs a dozen or seventy francs a hundred. They still weren't cheap – fifteen francs was four days' wages for a building worker, six days' wages for a miner, and eight days' wages for an agricultural worker – but they were immensely popular. In a few weeks after Prince Albert's death in 1861, Marion and Company of Regent Street sold over 70,000 *cartes-de-visite* of the Prince.

Cartes-de-visite were included in the first cricket book to be published containing photographs: *The Canterbury Cricket Week – an authentic narrative of the origin and career of the institution – including the programmes of the Old Stagers' performances, with the original prologues, epilogues, etc. spoken at each session.* This was published by W. Davey of Canterbury in 1865. The Grand Week at Canterbury was 'a gay and festive scene', according to the reporter for *The Field*: 'On Monday Kent met All England for the seventeenth time on the same tented field, and in the evening the old stagers appeared at the old theatre in Old Faces and New Pieces.

Tuesday was again devoted to the match in hand, and in the evening "amateur theatricals" were repeated at the Theatre Royal. Wedneday found the Gentlemen of Kent in opposition to I Zingari, after which a grand "cricket ball" took place at the New Music-hall, St Margaret's.'

W. Davey's *Canterbury Cricket Week* contained eight *cartes-de-visite* portraits of famous cricketers, stuck rather than printed in the book.

Surviving *cartes-de-visite* of H. Stephenson (by McLean and Company of London) and Richard Daft show clearly that such photographs were taken exclusively in the

studio, though that of Daft has at least a cricket background. Many *cartes-de-visite* were hand-coloured, including those dating back to 1870 of Jeremiah Coleman and F.C. Cobden. Coleman was a great supporter and patron of cricket: Cobden is remembered for what has passed into history as Cobden's Match. In the Varsity Match of 1870 at Lord's, Cobden bowled the over when Oxford needed only four runs to win with three wickets in hand. A single was scored from the first ball, and Cobden then took a hat-trick, to give Cambridge victory by two runs. The *carte-de-visite* dates from the same year.

From the mid-1860s onwards, most of the

XXII of Lansdown v The All England XI, Bath, 28-30 May 1863. One of the earlier photographs of 'the Doctor'. The group includes fourteen-year-old W.G. Grace (1) and twenty-one-year-old E.M. Grace (2). Source: The Roger Mann Collection

greatest names in cricket survive in photographs. We have little or no evidence of how they played – an off-drive by George Parr, Tom Hayward the Elder or E.M. Grace remains as much a figment of the imagination as the bowling action of Wisden or Pilch – but we can see how they were attired and equipped, and how they bore themselves. As yet, the laws of supply and demand had not been brought to bear on cricket photography. There was no sense that what was needed was a

shot of Edgar Willsher raising his arm above the shoulder when bowling (to settle once and for all whether Lillywhite had been right to no-ball him), and, even if there had been, the technology was not there to take the picture. Photography had come a long way since its dark beginnings over French rooftops, but it still needed time to catch up with the pace of the summer game. The next forty years were to see great developments in both the art and the sport.

A cricket match at the Mexico City Cricket Club c.1865.
Source: The Roger Mann Collection

CHAPTER 2

The Growth of Commercial Photography 1865-1914

'The future of illustrated journalism it is not easy to forecast.
Will the public get tired of photographs? I think not – while they are
able to convey with such intense reality many of the incidents of the hour.'
– Clement Shorter, Editor, Illustrated London News

B Y THE MID-1860s the 'artistic' amateur had been pushed aside by the professional photographer. No amateur could match the scope of the output of such enterprises as the London Stereoscope Company or the cheapness of the *cartes-de-visite*. In 1851 there were reckoned to be only fifty-one professional photographers in Britain: fifty years later that number had risen to 17,268. Photography was losing some of its romance. The camera became a recorder rather than a creator. There were, admittedly, some situations where it was hard to record, among them the agitated hurly-burly of sport and war, but technical advances allowed the camera to move nearer and nearer to the scene of action.

In 1842, *Punch* published a cartoon by John Leech. In the picture, a scruffy lad is standing inside a shop. The caption reads:

> *BOY AT NEWSAGENTS: I vants a*
> *nillustrated newspaper with a norrid*
> *murder and a likeness in it.*

In the early nineteenth century, newspapers were still expensive items, but one lesson learnt by the *Observer, Weekly Chronicle, Weekly Despatch* and *Bell's Life in London* was that the public were prepared to pay more for illustrated periodicals. The Coronation of George IV in 1821 had been celebrated in a special edition of the *Observer* that included four large engravings. In 1848, the *Illustrated London News* was launched as the world's first pictorial newspaper, in time for lavish picture coverage of the revolutions that swept Europe. John Gilbert, who worked for the *Illustrated London News,* was said to have produced over 30,000 drawings for that paper alone.

In 1869 – the same year that the illustrated weekly *The Graphic* saw light of day – *The Cricketer* was first published. It was a four-page broadsheet, giving fixture lists and match reports, entirely without illustration. The *Illustrated London News* carried engravings of the Derby and the Epsom Spring meeting, and on 22 June 1850 a 'Drawing of Cricket' by

W.G. Grace (1848-
1915). 'Mr Grace and his
brothers are men of
exceptional physique' –
The Saturday Review.
Source: The Hulton
Picture Company

The Right Reverend Henry Hutchinson Montgomery (1847-1932). He appeared for Harrow School Cricket XI (v Eton) 1864-66. He was Bishop of Tasmania 1889-1901, and in 1899 he wrote The History of Kennington & Its Neighbours *with chapters on cricket. His third son, Bernard Law, became Field Marshal, first Viscount Montgomery of Alamein. Source: Harrow School Archives*

Duncan. The artist depicted a scene similar to Fenton's early photograph – players in waistcoats, straw hats, a round arm bowler, a small tent under trees and a crowd gathered.

But cricket still received less coverage in such papers than racing, rowing, shooting or even chess. The big change came with the advent of mass-produced cricket photographs in *The Cricket and Football Times, Bicycling and Athletic Journal,* first published on 2 May 1878, price twopence. The photographs were not printed on the paper itself, but were *cartes-de-*

Jeremiah Coleman (Sir Jeremiah, JP) 1862-1942. Carte-de-visite, hand-coloured, 1870. A keen follower of cricket all his life. President of Surrey CCC 1916-22. He was known as the 'Mustard Millionaire'. His father founded the company of J & J Coleman. Source: Marylebone Cricket Club

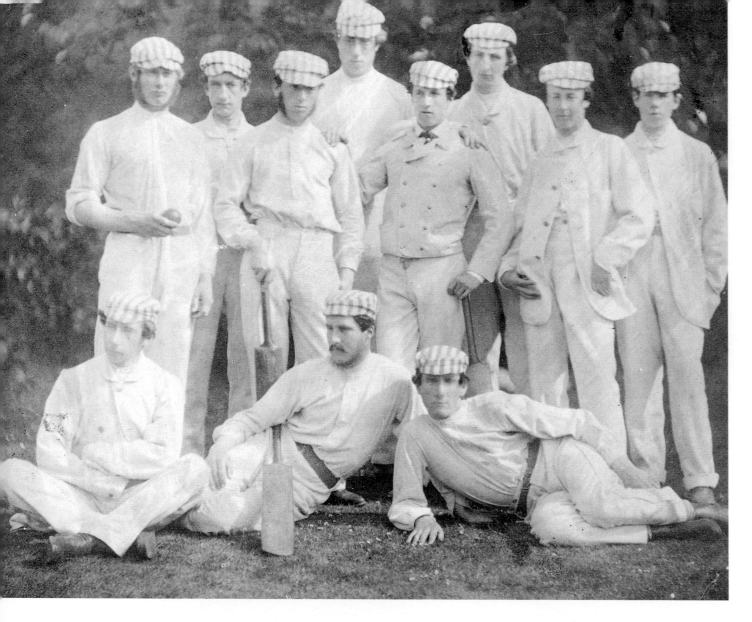

visite pasted on each copy. The first issue contained a photograph of the Queen's Park Football Club team on page three, but subsequent issues employed these photographs on the front cover. Apart from a special issue for September 1878, which contained a fine group photograph of the touring Australians shortly before their departure, it took two years for a cricketer to make an appearance – A. Shrewsbury on 3 June 1880, the picture credited to the London Stereoscopic Company. Soon after this, however, photographs disappeared from *The Cricket and Football Times*.

The Cricket Weekly Record, based in London, made its debut in May 1882 – in those days the season started later than it does today. In the first year of publication, its cover pictures consisted of poorly drawn portraits, mainly of

the visiting Australians. *The Cricket Field,* however, which began publication on 7 May 1892, used real photographs on its cover, the first issue carrying a large portrait of W.G. Grace. Issue No. 2 had a cover picture of Lord Hawke's team in waterproof boiler suits and sou'westers standing beneath Niagara Falls during their tour of North America. The next three issues contained, respectively, studio portraits of Alfred Shaw, Mr John Shuter ('from a photo by Mr Lavender, Bromley, Kent'), and Mr A.J. Webbe, the Middlesex opening bat ('from a photo by Messrs Hawkins and Co., Brighton'). Apart from portraits, team photographs were still very much the order of the day: William Nofman's picture of the Gentlemen Cricketers who played in America in 1872 (among them Grace and Hornby); the swaggeringly posed United South of England Eleven of 1871; or the wonderful shot of James Lillywhite's Test pioneers, taken at Priory Park, Chichester a few days before they sailed for Australia in the autumn of 1876. Occasionally, a photographer would pull off a coup without realising it. In 1870, an unknown cameraman took a photo of the Notts team, including George Summers. A few days later, Summers had the misfortune to become the first cricketer to be killed in a first-class match.

It was with the coming of cheap illustrated daily newspapers (*Daily Mail, Daily Mirror, Sketch* and *Daily Graphic*) that cricket photography first became regularly available for mass consumption. The reader was still years away from seeing close-up action photography, but, by the turn of the century, cricketers were no longer bound to the studio for photographic

representation. The *Daily Mirror* for 29 April 1904 had pictures of Lord Dalmeny and W.G. on its front page, to celebrate the opening of the season, and the following day published a picture of the match between London County and Surrey in action. The caption read: 'Lockwood, at the far wicket, has just hit a boundary for Surrey'. By 1906 photographs were being incorporated within the text, rather than appearing as a miscellaneous montage in a special spread. The issue for 30 April 1907 devoted the whole of its front page to the opening of the season at the Oval, with pictures of C.F. Reiner, captain of the Next Sixteen practising in the nets, Hayward and Hobbs walking out to bat, Surrey cricketers taking the field, and Jackson 'loosening his arms' at the nets.

That same year *The Cricketer and Football*

The United South of England XI, Chichester 1871. Back, left to right: E. Pooley, John Lillywhite, G. Griffith, T. Humphrey, F. Silcock, James Lillywhite (Jun). Middle, left to right: H. Charlwood, G.F. Grace, W.G. Grace, J. Southerton. Front, left to right: H. Jupp, R. Humphrey. In those days, cricketers presented their impedimenta to the camera – almost as proof of their trade. Source: West Sussex Records Office/Priory Park Cricket Club

James Lillywhite (Jun) and the England cricketers at Chichester a few days before their departure to Australia and New Zealand 1876-77. Standing left to right: H. Jupp, T. Emmett, A. Hobgen, A. Hill, T. Armitage. Seated left to right: E. Pooley, J. Southerton, J. Lillywhite (Jun), A. Shaw, G. Ulyett, A. Greenwood. Front left to right: H.Charlwood, J. Selby. Arthur Hobgen, a member of the Priory Park Cricket Club, financed the tour. Source: Marylebone Cricket Club

Player was first published on 7 June, price one penny. This magazine not only used photographs but also was one of the first to show a sense of design in the use it made of photographs. The pictures of H. Lees (Surrey), 're-arranging his slips', and The Doctor (W.G.), 'placing his field', were presented side by side, turning in towards each other, giving a sense of balance and symmetry.

The older *Cricket* magazine was first published in 1882, but made very conservative use of photographs until Archie MacLaren's editorship in the summer of 1914. By then the quality of cricket photographs had improved enormously, and the range of cricket subjects was greatly extended. Three books in particular chart this progress: C.W. Alcock and Richard W. Thomas's *Famous Cricketers and Cricket Grounds* (1895), C.B. Fry's *The Book of Cricket* (1899), and Ranjitsinhji's *Jubilee Book of Cricket* (1897). Although some of Alcock and

Thomas's pictures were studio-based, many are memorably beautiful and have been subsequently reproduced dozens of times – that of Rhodes with deceptively soft eyes for such a canny cricketer, or the picture of Jessop, leaning on a pavilion balcony, with no trace of the aggression that brought him 26,698 runs in his career at an average of eighty runs an hour.

In all this the photographer gradually replaced the artist in illustrated journals, magazines and newspapers. The period is concurrent with the career of the most famous cricketer of all time: W.G. Grace. The Doctor was one of the greatest of Victorian personalities. In the words of a song from the *All England Cricket and Football Journal*:

> *Britannia may gladly be proud of her sons,*
> *Since who is more famous than he,*
> *The stalwart compiler of thousands of runs,*
> *'Leviathan' W.G.?*

He was a celebrity, in the modern sense of the word. It has been said that he and Queen Victoria were the two people who would have been instantly recognised by most of the population a hundred or so years ago. That any public figure could be so readily identified says much for the power and popularity of photography.

In the forty-three years of Grace's career, cricket came of age. The modern county championship was instituted, Test matches began, statistics approached a degree of sophistication, *Wisden* began publication, the science of batting, bowling and fielding developed, the present day 'centres of excellence' were created. And we see

something of Grace in all of this. There are photographs of him watching cricket, walking out to bat, returning to the pavilion (usually in a benign frame of mind – it's a shame that the camera never caught him in one of his explosive moments when wrongly adjudged leg before), coaching, demonstrating, practising, and occupying the captain's place in many group pictures. There are even one or two photographs of Grace playing, but from a distance. With shutter speeds of up to one-thousandth of a second, the camera could now capture action, but lacked the telephoto lens that would bring the action close enough.

So we have to make do with pictures of Grace in relative repose and calm. Nonetheless,

The Australian team in England in 1878 – a very beautiful example of a hand-coloured photograph. Standing, left to right: F.R. Spofforth, J. Conway (Manager), F.E. Allen. Middle, left to right: G.H. Bailey, T.P. Horan, T.W. Garrett, D.W. Gregory (capt), A.C. Bannerman, H.F. Boyle. Front, left to right: C.Bannerman, W.L. Murdoch, J.M. Blackham. Source: Marylebone Cricket Club

his career is well documented by the camera – if nothing else, we can see how the slim athlete, who topped the English batting averages twelve seasons out of fifteen from 1866 to 1880, steadily grew into the stout Grand Old Man of the early 1900s. The portrait of him in 1880, bat under his arm, eyes straight to camera, muscular right arm by his side, is powerful and impressive. And if he did put on weight later in life, his increased bulk had its advantages. One Nottinghamshire bowler remarked late in life to Cardus: 'His big body med th' wickets look so little that you felt the ball weren't big enough'. Grace bowed out of first-class cricket in the cold spring of 1908, but he was still a formidable force. Three years earlier, he had been featured in Beldam and Fry's *Great Batsmen*, indeed the book was itself dedicated to Grace, 'The King of Cricket'.

Again, it should be remembered that neither cricket nor photography was confined to the Test playing nations. *The Strand* magazine of 1898 carried an article on 'Savage Cricketers' by

ABOVE: *J.M. Blackham (1854-1932). Often known as the 'Prince' of Australian wicketkeepers he went on every one of the first eight tours made by the Australians to England between 1878 and 1893.*
Source: The Hulton Picture Company
RIGHT: *W.G. Grace founded the London County Cricket Club in 1900. They enjoyed first-class-cricket status and played sides from the clubs, counties and visiting touring sides. The club seemed to give Grace a new lease of cricketing life at the age of fifty-two.*
Source: Aerofilms

The interval, Lord's, 1908. The photograph was taken by Horace W. Nicholls (1867-1941) whose work included the coverage of the Second Boer War (1899-1902) and the scenes, events and people of the Edwardian era. He worked as a photographer with the Imperial War Museum during the First World War (1914-18). Source: The Royal Photographic Society, Bath

William C. Fitzgerald, illustrated with photographs of cricket being played in the Solomon Islands, Uganda, Northern Ceylon and New Guinea. In 1880, Fred Kruger ('Gold Medallist of Geelong, Victoria') took a fine picture of Aborigines playing cricket at the Coranderrk Station, Healesville, and two years earlier one of the few real action shots was taken of the game between The Army and the Melbourne Cricket Club at the MCG.

Throughout this period, hand–colouring of photographs continued to be popular, and a fine example exists in that of the Australian touring party of 1878. The Aboriginal team that toured in 1868 were well covered by the camera. There are photgraphs of the ship they sailed in (the *Parramatta*), of them playing at Derby, and of them posed outside a cricket tent. Ten years later, however, there was even more extensive picture coverage of the first official Australian team. 'Not until Monday, 27 May 1878 did the English public take any interest in Australian cricket,' wrote A.G. Steel,

that being the day 4000 people saw MCC thrashed by nine wickets at Lord's, Spofforth returning a match analysis of 10 for 20. It is said that at least one MCC member believed all the Australians would be black, until they appeared before him. Photography did much to educate as well as entertain.

The camera was becoming more and more mobile. Team photographs could be set up far more quickly, and taken during the lunch or tea interval. The Brownie camera had arrived, allowing snapshots to be taken by the thousand, including the fine picture of W.G. and F.S. Jackson at the Oval in 1905, that of Lebrun Constantine and A.E. Harrigan in May 1906, and that of the Eton captain, H.S. Hatfield leading his admirers to the pavilion in 1907.

Cricket photographs became less formal. Pictures of teams taking or leaving the field have a sense of moment and movement, arms swing jauntily, some heads are down, conversations are clearly taking place. The camera is no longer merely recording an

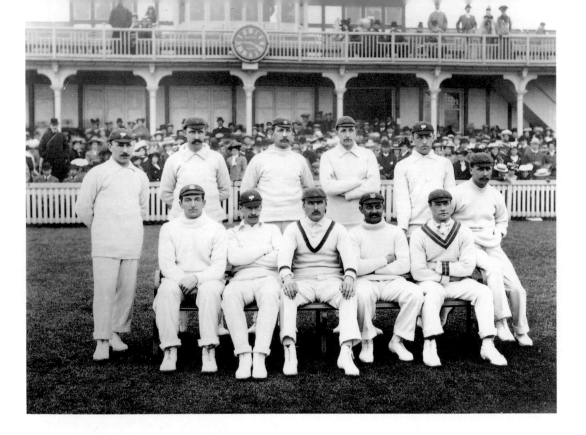

The England XI (v Australia) Edgbaston, 1902. The photograph was taken by Thomas Lewis (1844-1913). Back row, left to right: G.H. Hirst, A.F.A. Lilley, W.H. Lockwood, L.C. Braund, W. Rhodes, J.T. Tyldesley. Front row, left to right: C.B. Fry, F.S. Jackson, A.C. MacLaren (capt.), K.S. Ranjitsinhji, G.L.Jessop. Source: John Whybrow Collection

The second West Indian Team to visit England 1906 (the first was in 1900). Back row, left to right: G.C. Learmond, J.J. Cameron, C.K. Bancroft, C.S. Morrison. Middle row, left to right: S.G. Smith, L.S. Constantine, P.A. Goodman, R.A. Ollivierre. Front row, left to right: G. Challenor, O.H. Layne, J.E. Parker, H.B.G. Austin (capt), R.H. Mallett (Manager), C.P. Cumberbatch. L.S. Constantine (1874-1942) was the father of Learie (Lord) Constantine (1901-71). Source: Marylebone Cricket Club

Dr W.G.Grace (1848-1915) and Rt. Hon. F.S. Jackson (1870-1947). An inscription on the photograph reads 'A Kodak snapshot taken by A.P.Grace'. The photograph was taken possibly in 1905 when Jackson was captain of England (v Australia). Kodak Limited, in those days, bought photographs of people in the news to put on display in their shops and outlets. Source: Marylebone Cricket Club

artificially posed scene, but is capturing an incident on a summer day, preserving for ever one of those scenes that seem eternal to cricket, as in the shots of Grace and his London County team of 1900, or of Hobbs and MacLaren going out to bat against Australia at Edgbaston on 28 May 1909. Within half an hour, both were back in the pavilion, victims of Macartney – MacLaren for 5, Hobbs for 0.

But, pictorially as well as statistically, the age belonged to Grace. His likeness was to be seen in newspapers, magazines, books, pamphlets, posters, programmes – always the centre of gravity of any team picture; often watching cricket; sometimes well away from the cricket field, hunting, or playing golf or tennis. A picture of a late Victorian summer without W.G. Grace is unimaginable.

CHAPTER 3

The Rise
of Action
Photography

*'If you cannot see at a glance that the old game is up,
that the camera has hopelessly beaten the pencil and paintbrush
as an instrument of artistic representation, then you will never make a true critic:
you are only, like most critics, a picture fancier.'*
– George Bernard Shaw, 1901

THE MAN generally credited as the 'Father of Motion Photography' is Eadweard (or Edward) Muybridge (or Muggeridge), who was born in Kingston-upon-Thames in 1830, but who later emigrated to the United States, where he worked in New York with the daguerreotypist Silas Selleck (or Helios). Muybridge was a strange man, with a mad look about him, not unlike Ben Gunn on a bad day. He was also an occasionally violent man, who was tried for killing his wife's lover, one Major Henry Larkyns, but was acquitted on the grounds of justifiable homicide. He also made a photographic trip to the Far West, taking over 2000 photographs, before returning to the East Coast, obsessed with the idea of capturing what he called 'Animal Motion' with the camera. There is a story that his experiments in this field enabled him to supply Leland Stanford, Governor of California and President of the Central Pacific Railroad, with evidence to win a bet that a galloping horse did, at times, have all four feet off the ground.

Muybridge's technique for action photography was simple. A series of trip wires, broken in succession, fired off a line of cameras, giving one still shot for each second or so of movement. By 1877, Muybridge was using a shutter capable of firing at one-thousandth of a second, and as his technique improved, using electronically controlled shutters, Muybridge was able to take rapid series of photographs with so little change in position from one to the other that they resemble the component pictures of a flicker book. In 1884, he received a grant of $40,000 from the University of Pennsylvania which helped him complete his best-known work *The Human Figure in Motion, An Electro-Photographic Investigation of Consecutive Phases of Muscular Actions*. This was a collection of dozens of photographic spreads showing series of pictures of men and women performing various actions – walking, stooping, running, picking something up. Among the spreads were those of an athlete running and picking up a ball (wearing only a student cap), a

J.B. Hobbs (Sir John)
Surrey and England
(1882-1963) – one of
the finest 'posed' action
pictures ever taken, and
used in coaching manuals.
Source: Press Association

Eadweard Muybridge (1830-1904) pioneered the use of a number of cameras to produce sequential photographs. His model for these photographs was 'the best all-round cricketer in the University of Pennsylvania' and appeared in The Human Figure in Motion *published in 1887. Source: Victoria & Albert Museum Picture Library*

totally naked athlete catching a ball (and dropping it), and a soldier on guard (marching up and down carrying rifle and bayonet, and wearing only a jock strap). Surprisingly, there was also a naked cricketer, reputedly 'the best all-round cricketer in the University of Pennsylvania'. This first streaker managed to keep a straight face as well as a straight bat as he demonstrated the straight-drive.

Towards the end of the nineteenth century, the development of the high-speed shutter and a great improvement in the quality of lenses meant that genuine action shots of cricket could at last be taken. Many of the so-called 'action' shots were posed, but others are real enough. And the great value attached to such

photography was that it enabled a detailed analysis to be made of the ways cricketers moved. Thanks to Beldam, Rouch and others, the enthusiast could now see how Fry and Trumper, Hobbs and Ranji used their arms, wrists, legs and feet. It was possible to catch Tom Richardson in mid-air, to study what Cardus so beautifully described: 'His action moved one like music because it was so rhythmical. He ran to the wicket a long distance, and at the bowling creases his terminating leap made you catch breath.'

In 1896 Archie MacLaren published his *Cricket for Beginners,* which contained twenty-three photographs of MacLaren himself. The aim of the book was to help aspiring

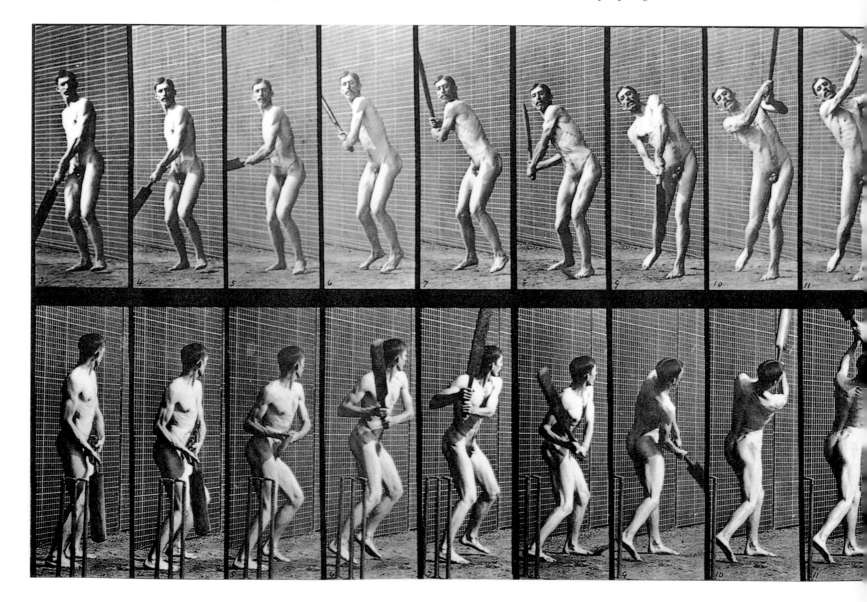

youngsters. The camera had become a teaching tool, and the illustrations showed 'Position at Wicket', 'Position as Bowler Delivers the Ball', 'Forward Play', 'Pulling the Straight Ball', etc. Each picture was accompanied by a qualifying 'Good' or 'Bad'. There were no photographs of bowling or fielding, and, although they were intended to give an idea of real cricket strokes, none of the pictures had a sense of movement.

The Beldam and Fry books are central to the history of cricket photography for at least three reasons. The quality of the photographs is excellent. The subjects chosen (Grace, Ranji, Trumper, Clem Hill, Archie MacLaren, M.A. Noble, Hirst, J.T. Tyldesley, Jessop, Quaife, Perrin, J.H. Sinclair, et al) were the greatest players of one of cricket's greatest Golden Ages. The book showed a commitment to the whole notion of cricket photography. It was, said the authors, 'a genuine attempt to present things as they are and batsmen as they play...In short, the book is founded upon Action-Photography and Actual Experience.'

The books were intended, at least in part, as coaching manuals. 'Action-Photography is of value since it shows in full detail the various stages in a stroke, and thus betrays secrets which the human eye cannot detect.' In 1900, five years before the book was published, Fry had written of Ranjitsinhji: 'There is that in his strokes that baffles the most confident analyst. One feels inclined to say..."Come on, Ranji,

Essex v Australians, Leyton, May 1909. C.P. Buckenham bowls to V.T. Trumper. Trumper scored 74 and Buckenham took 3-154 in the Australians total of 609.

Source: The Roger Mann Collection

this isn't cricket, it's infernal juggling".' Once the photographs had been taken, Beldam and Fry thought that the camera disproved the theory that there was something magically different about Ranji's technique: 'But he has a more subtle and more supple manner of moving; he moves as if he had no bones.' In the case of George Hirst, they described one of his highly individual shots thus: 'He jumps in front of his wicket with both feet together so that he is facing the bowler, and lets fly at the ball with a full horizontal sweep of the bat, which, if the stroke is carefully timed, as it usually is, drives the ball to square leg. Needless to say this is a stroke which the ordinary batsman may admire with despair and imitate at his peril.' W.G. Quaife is singled out as perhaps the best model: 'A.C. MacLaren's off-drive, Victor Trumper's cut, G.L. Jessop's pull, are magnificent strokes played by these men, but to copy them might be dangerous. W.G. Quaife's strokes might be imitated with an absolute assurance that if the imitations were correct, so, too, would be the stroke, no matter what the build or physical characteristics of the imitator.' Interestingly, the captions relating to the photographs of Fry are very critical of technique. Presumably they were written by Fry himself.

The undertaking had its moments of both humour and danger. The stock bowlers employed by Beldam and Fry couldn't always produce the right ball for the stroke being photographed, and there were times when one of the Gods of the Golden Age executed a perfect off-drive to a long hop outside the leg stump, the camera faithfully and embarrassingly capturing the ball as it passed by on the other side. Sometimes, Beldam himself bowled, releasing the camera shutter by means of a long cable held in his left hand. This meant that he had to discipline himself to control three disparate movements within a very short time: bowling accurately, firing off the camera, and taking evasive action if the ball was hit in his direction.

Nobody turned down a request to take part.

The project was supported by the county clubs as well as the individual cricketers, and Beldam travelled to many grounds in search of his subjects. One county secretary asked how long it would take Beldam to photograph each member of his club in action. When Beldam explained that each exposure lasted one-thousandth of a second, the Secretary was much relieved, and remarked: 'Oh, well, then, you'll soon be through with our eleven.'

The books include an interesting essay by Beldam on 'Timing With The Camera', in which he compares timing as a batsman and timing as a photographer. 'The power to time with the camera depends upon the same

K.S.Ranjitsinhji (1872-1933). The Leg Glance. 'Suddenly he found out that by moving the left leg across towards the off, keeping his bat on the leg side of it and facing the ball quite squarely with his body, he could watch the ball on the bat and play it away to leg with a twist of the wrist.'
– C.B. Fry, 1900.
Source: The George Beldam Collection

G.W. Beldam (1868-1937) combined an expert knowledge of cricket (Middlesex and Gentlemen) and photography to produce an outstanding series of analytical photographs showing the players of the Edwardian era – one of the 'Golden Ages' of cricket. They are to be seen in two books Great Batsmen – Their Methods at a Glance *(1905) and* Great Bowlers – Their Methods at a Glance *(1906) with written commentary by C.B. Fry (1872-1956).*
F.S. Jackson (1870-1947). The Straight Drive.
Source: The George Beldam Collection

qualities of eye, brain and hand as does skill in games. It is the power of concentration and sympathy with every movement of the player, as seen focused on a reflector, that are the real secrets of timing with the camera...Indeed, it is essential to success that the eye should unconsciously anticipate every movement, otherwise part of the stroke required would be missed and another part taken, possibly out of focus.' Further, Beldam was at pains to emphasise the integrity of his work: 'The block-makers have not touched the ball where

C. Blythe (1879-1917). The Beginning of the Swing. A typical Beldam study. Source: The George Beldam Collection

One of the most famous cricket photographs of all time. V.T. Trumper (1877-1915). The Straight Drive. 'Spoil a bowler's length and you've got him' – Trumper.
Source: The George Beldam Collection

it is seen in the picture, and everything in the reproductions is identical with the negatives...any such re-touching of the ball would be against the spirit of instantaneous photography.'

In 1924, MacLaren published another book, *Cricket Old and New – A Straight Talk to Young Players*. This contained twenty-five photographs, mainly from the London News Agency, Sport & General Press and W. Hawkins. Two of the pictures are more interesting than the general run of Beldam or sub-Beldam types. These are

of 'throwing in' and are captioned as coming from 'cinema film'. MacLaren again wished his book and his pictures to train aspiring youngsters: 'I have very seldom seen a cricketer practising the throw-in. The Australian players will frequently throw a full pitch from the boundary to the wicket-keeper, a feat I have never seen performed by any of our own men.'

Two years later came a more important work, also by MacLaren, *The Perfect Batsman – J.B. Hobbs in Action*, 'with ninety-eight Cinema-Photographs of J.B. Hobbs at the Wicket'.

Three separate photographs of S.J. Santall of Warwickshire (1873-1957) when placed together show the sequence of his bowling action. This had been noticed by Ken Kelly and published in his book Cricket Reflections. *The photographer was W.A. Rouch, an important pioneer of sports photography, whose family ran a business in London designing and making cameras. The photographs originally appeared in* The Book of Cricket *by C.B.Fry, published in 1899.*

Australia v England, second Test match, Melbourne, December 1912-January 1913. W. Rhodes (61) batting during England's first innings. A. Cotter is the bowler and J.W. Hearne is the non-strike batsman. The camera is still far from the action. Source: The Hulton Picture Company

'The batsman of these pictures is the 1914 Hobbs who could then reduce good length bowling to a state of impotency, from the very commencement of his innings, just as Victor Trumper did...if we could find half a dozen batsmen half as good as him (Hobbs) when these pictures were taken for me by Messrs Cherry Kearton Limited, we would not be long in scoring big totals against this Australian Eleven of 1926...Hobbs is the youngest batsman for his age I have ever seen, and his alteration in his play today, compared with the season of 1914, when these pictures were taken, is very slight, and only perceptible to those who understand the finer points of batting.'

The photographs consisted of a series of plates, each containing eight, ten or twelve frames, showing a range of strokes: 'Drive to mid-off along the ground', 'A Change from Attack to Defence', 'A Square Cut to a Ball on the Short Side', etc. All the pictures were taken at the Oval, during a season in which Hobbs hit ten centuries, including three doubles. This was not, however, the first time a cine-camera had been to a cricket match, or even to the Oval. In August 1902, Mr R.W. Paul of 60 High Holborn obtained permission from the

Gentlemen v Players,
Lord's, July 1887.
General view looking
towards the Grand Stand.
A. Shrewsbury (Players)
is batting during his
innings of 111. W.G.
Grace is fielding at mid-
off. He scored 24 and 49
and took 5-116. The
Players won by an innings
and 123 runs.
Source: Marylebone
Cricket Club

Surrey Club to take pictures of Test and other matches for a fee of ten guineas a day, as long as the play and the view of spectators were not interfered with. And a cine-camera was certainly at Lord's in 1898 for the match between the Gentlemen and Players. There is a sequence showing Grace, Shrewsbury and William Gunn leading a group of players along a path just behind a bank of spectators, reckoned to be on the site of what is now the Warner Stand.

Two editions of *The Badminton Library – Cricket* (another book that began life in magazine form) show something of the

development of action cricket photography. The first edition, published in 1904, has the standard posed shots of Beldam, but the second edition of 1920, uses several photographs taken by Central News photographers during the 1919 season. As well as a fine shot of A.W. Carr hooking, there are three great catches: J.W. Hearne at cover point, catching Denton inches from the ground during the Middlesex v Yorkshire match at Lord's; Woolley at second slip, catching Kilner during the Champion County v England match at the Oval; and D.J. Knight also at second slip, catching an unnamed Yorkshire batsman during their match with

Surrey, again at the Oval.

For the camera was moving ever closer to the action. The general view of Lord's during the Gentlemen v Players game, 11 July 1887, is taken from too great a distance for us to be even certain of the score on the board. Twenty-five years later, during the triangular Test series of 1912, much more is revealed. There are action photographs of the Australian and England teams practising in the nets at the Oval, and in the shots of the actual matches, it is now possible to identify the players. The previous winter, the atmosphere at the vast Melbourne ground was captured as never before, during the triumphant tour of J.W.H.T. Douglas and the England party.

One of the best action sequences of this early period is that taken by W.A. Rouch in 1899 of the comparatively little-known Warwickshire bowler, Sidney J. Santall, who was usually brought on as first change after the openers had achieved little. The photographs are perhaps the first to give a sense of the

enormous physical effort that goes into bowling, superior to anything that went before and much of what came after. Beldam's shots of Richardson, Rhodes, Spofforth, Lockwood, Bosanquet et al look tame in comparison. Rouch's photographs of Santall have been described as 'possibly the first ever bowling sequence pictures', but there is some uncertainty as to whether we are looking at three separate deliveries, or one delivery covered by three cameras. Rouch was a professional photographer who was something of a sports specialist.

By the 1920s action photography was almost commonplace and team photographs were beginning to take on a more disciplined appearance, as that of the visiting Australian tourists of 1921 shows. Shots of the Hon. L.H. Tennyson batting for Hampshire against the almost all-conquering Australians, of Brown of Hampshire (who made his Test debut in the summer of 1921, keeping wicket at Headingley, Old Trafford and the Oval, and

England v Australia, first Test match, Edgbaston, 1909. A.C. MacLaren and J.B. Hobbs open for England. This was Hobbs' first Test match appearance in England and his scores were 0 and 62 not out.
Source: The Hulton Picture Company

The Australians at Leicester for the first match of their tour in 1921. Back row, left to right: S. Smith (Manager), J. Ryder, J.M. Gregory, H.S.T.L. Hendry, E.A. McDonald, A.A. Mailey. Front row, left to right: W. Bardsley, C.G. Macartney, W.W. Armstrong (capt.), H.L. Collins, H. Carter, J.M. Taylor, T.J.E. Andrews. Source: Press Association

Hon. L.H. Tennyson (1889-1951) batting against the bowling of J.M. Gregory. H. Carter is the wicketkeeper and C.G. Macartney is fielding. This photograph was probably taken during the third Test match between England and Australia, Leeds, 1921. Tennyson had taken over the captaincy of England from J.W.H.T. Douglas and scored 63 and 36 despite an injured hand. After the First World War, bigger lenses brought the action nearer. Source: Press Association

scoring 250 runs for an average of 50.00), of Macartney's century at Headingley, and of Woolley batting at the Oval, are still powerful images. Even better, perhaps, are the pictures of Fender the following summer – putting Hampshire to the sword in early May, when he scored 185 in two hours and ten minutes, and toiling heroically in what *Wisden* described as 'the sensation of the season at the Oval'.

Even the posed action shots were an improvement on earlier studies. That of Hobbs jumping out to drive, though lacking the authenticity of real-life cricket drama, is a

wonderful study of power and elegance. The huge backlift and the dancing feet, the athletic figure and the face to camera, combine to produce a photograph that is one of the best of The Master ever taken. It is possible to believe in this picture. This is not a man posing for the camera, but the greatest batsman in the world revealing a little of his brilliance. This is the man who, in the words of H.S. Altham, was often tempted 'to try dangerous strokes because the mere making of runs by ordinary secure means had begun to pall...' And this is the man whose career began where Grace's left off.

F.E. Woolley (1887-1978) of Kent and England. He is seen batting against the Australians.
W.A. Oldfield, wicket-keeper, J.M. Gregory, slip, and H.L. Collins in the covers.
Source: The Hulton Picture Company

CHAPTER 4

Photography
and the
Printed Page

'Newspaper photography was the first means whereby
the man in the street came into direct visual contact
with the world in which he lived.'
— Tom Hopkinson

IMPROVEMENTS in the techniques and equipment used in cricket photography had a considerable effect on cricket writing. In the first place, easy access to photographs led to an increased demand for educative and informative books on how to bat, bowl or field. The works of Beldam and Fry, Archie MacLaren and P.F. Warner (who edited *The Badminton Library – Cricket*), clearly fall into this category. Secondly, photography changed the way in which people wrote about cricket. Until the arrival of the action photograph, cricket writers had a recording monopoly. Words provided the only means of capturing a bludgeoning hook shot or a rasping drive. Cricket reports were lengthy affairs, running to two or three broadsheet columns of small print in the case of Test matches, and affording the writer a chance to be profligate in his account. The report in *Wisden* of the game between Oxford and Cambridge in 1877 ran to almost 3000 words. *The Times* needed over 2000 words to describe the final day's play of the Oval Test in September 1880. In a report of a match between the Australians and Sussex in July 1899, it took seventy-five very ordinary words to describe how Trumper dealt with a ball pitched up on his legs. In the words of Cardus: 'Whoever would not be spendthrift of language about Trumper, let him not write on him at all'.

Once the camera was capable of freezing a catch, a shot, or the leap of a fast bowler at the point of delivery, many of these thousands of words became redundant. It is a process that has gone on and on, forcing writers on cricket to deal more and more with the inner, invisible workings of the game. The camera has taken so much away from the typewriter that the contemporary cricket writer spends most of his time describing the state of the pitch and the crowd, speculating on the prognoses for those injured and the outcome of the game, and analysing the motives behind electing to field or making bowling changes. Television has obviously hastened this process, but even a

W. Rhodes (1877-1973). 'Every ball looked exactly alike. Every ball was different. On a bad wicket... a batsman would feel like the hero of an Edgar Allan Poe story.' – A.A. Thomson. Source: Hulton Picture Company

verbal medium such as radio devotes most of its time to comment, surmise and chatter. There is now such a vast legacy of cricket images in our memories, culled from photographs, that we need not be told how any but the most eccentric cricketers bat, bowl or field.

By the end of the nineteenth century, so long as they had access to books and papers, most people would have been able to recognise top cricketers. Cricket had the great advantage over other sports in that it contained long periods of seeming inactivity. It was there, in all its stationary glory, to be captured by the box on the tripod. With cricket, there was no

need – yet – for the photographer to panic. Photographs in papers, magazines and books were still enough of a novelty for the public to be happy with portraits, team pictures and the occasional distant view of a match in progress.

And more and more journals and books were including photographs. *Wisden* first used photographs in the 1889 edition, with a single page of photographs of the 'Six Great Bowlers of the Year 1888'. 'Our portraits are from fresh negatives by the well-known Brighton firm of E. Hawkins and Co., who have made cricket photography their speciality.' The following year, *Wisden* featured 'Nine Great Batsmen'

The XXII of Easingwold and District (v North of England XI) at Easingwold, Yorkshire, 28-30 June 1870. Photograph by Johnson of Bradford and Shipley. Source: The Roger Mann Collection

W.G. Grace makes a donation during a charity cricket match in 1915. The camera was beginning to seek informal pictures. Source: Press Association

BELOW: *K.S.Ranjitsinhji (HH Shri Sir Ranjitsinhji Vibhaji, Jam Sahib of Nawanagar) at the funeral of W.G. Grace, 1915. Source: Press Association*

and, in the 1891 edition, 'Five Great Wicket-Keepers'.

The camera was making cricketers famous and familiar. The public were beginning to look forward to photographs of their favourites. In 1897 *Wisden* recorded: 'As regards the photographs for the present issue of WISDEN'S ALMANACK, the choice this year was a very simple one. Before the season was many weeks old, it was perfectly clear that Ranjitsinhji's portrait would have to be given, and with the Australians gradually winning back the position that had been lost during the four previous tours, it was soon arranged that the most successful batsman and bowler in the team should appear in the picture. To complete the five players, the choice fell upon Richardson and Lilley, of neither of whom had a portrait been previously published in the ALMANACK.' And so was born the 'Five Cricketers of the Season' (in textual terms) or 'of the Year' (in photographic terms), and the first to be honoured were Ranji, Richardson, Lilley, Trumble and S.E. Gregory.

Once again the photographs were the work of Hawkins of Brighton, though it has to be said that the early illustrations in *Wisden* were poor affairs, tiny fingernail-size portraits, faintly reproduced, with little to suggest that these were men of action. It took a long time for *Wisden* to change. Not until 1938 were photographs other than The Five Cricketers of the Year included. Copiously illustrated, by contrast, was Percy Cross Standing's *Cricket Yesterday and Today*, published in two volumes in 1902 in a subscription edition. The text was by experts – Abel on batting, Rhodes on bowling, A.O. Jones on fielding – and redolent of the age in which it was written. 'Why is the fielder of today so greatly inferior to that of former times?' wrote Jones. 'The answer can be summed up in a very few words. He is too lazy to practise.' The photographs, however, show a considerable advance on much that had gone before. There is a photograph of Clem Hill, standing in front of the massive Adelaide scoreboard on 19 December 1900 after scoring 365 not out for South Australia v New South Wales, and one of the crowd in front of the Oval pavilion at the end of the 1896 Test. There are also action photographs of Oxford v Cambridge 1901, the first Test at Sydney in 1901, the second Test at Melbourne, the third Test at Adelaide in 1902, and of cricket in Portugal and the United States.

A much later work by Percy Cross Standing – *Anglo-Australian Cricket 1862-1926* – shows how cricket photography already had a sense of

its own history by the mid-1920s. The book contains sixteen photographs, many of them by Lionel Wood, another Brighton-based photographer. While the early pictures of Jackson, MacLaren, Fry, Ranji and company are the familiar old posed collection, there is a fine shot of Collins and Bardsley walking out to open the innings against Leicestershire on the first match of the Australians' 1921 tour. Only the camera could capture such a moment so well. A photograph could show so much more, and by the First World War people were beginning to collect cricket photographs, and the public was starting to take cricket photography almost for granted.

The amount of cricket photography had, of course, been greatly increased by newspapers and magazines, and more and more aspects of the game were covered by the camera. Press photographers were at the ground well before the start of play, capturing the formalities that took place before battle commenced. There is a fine picture of Armstrong and Douglas in front of the pavilion at Trent Bridge, about to toss in the one hundredth Test between England and Australia. The benches behind the captains are already full, every head covered by trilby, boater or cap, and a schoolboy leans eagerly

Jack Hobbs signing autographs during his benefit match – Surrey v Kent – the Oval, 1919. The camera now followed cricketers off the field of play.
Source: Press Association

P.G.H. Fender (1892-1985) of Surrey batting against Hampshire, May 1922. He scored 185. The wicketkeeper is S. Fry (son of C.B. Fry). Source: Press Association

forward, staring at his heroes. The picture tells us something of the enormous popularity of cricket in the first half of this century, and the cameramen were now equipped to meet the great appetite for photographic coverage of the national sport. The camera faithfully recorded England's defeat, including the bizarre and horrendous moment when poor Ernest Tyldesley 'played on' with his face. The 'incident' fast became one of the most prized shots from any cricket match.

As cricket became more and more popular, and as photography became more and more adept at capturing the game, editors and readers pressed for an increase in the scope of pictorial cricket coverage. The public wanted to know far more of the details of the lives of their heroes off the field. Leading cricketers were hot, in more ways than one. Cameramen were sent to get pictures of players off duty and off guard. Photographs were published of players signing autographs, of crowds strolling round the pitch during an interval in play or of scenes of joy at the end of a match.

More and more people attended cricket matches, and more and more photographs were

taken of the game, so more and more books were written about the subject, many of them illustrated. A Fred Buchanan cartoon poked fun at the number of players who had turned author; by 1910 many cricketers were earning extra money in this way. One of the earliest to do so was E.H.D. Sewell, the Essex amateur, who wrote for the *Daily Graphic* and was a keen photographer. These photographs were used in books of cricket reminiscences and anecdotes that he subsequently published in the 1930s and 1940s. *Cricket Up to Date,* published in 1931, contains a photograph of W.G. Grace

and W.L. Murdoch taken by Sewell on Grace's fifty-sixth birthday, at Coventry on 18 July 1904, one of A.C. MacLaren and Ranji 'in the Jamsaheb's garden at Staines', an excellent photograph of Hobbs, and others of Tate, White, Chapman, Rhodes and Perrin. There is also a photograph of Sewell himself, illustrating 'the correct stance as the author believes it should be'. The whole tone of the book is Colonel Blimpish in style, advocating a return to the old days and old ways – including the five ball over – and warning of the dangers that threatened cricket. 'I suppose it would be

P.G.H. Fender of Surrey bowling during the match against Kent at the Oval, July 1922. His match figures included 137 and 4-75. It was also the benefit match for T. Rushby of Surrey. Source: Press Association

Test Trial Match,
England v The Rest,
Trent Bridge, May 1924.
The England team take
the field. Left to right,
R. Kilner, H. Sutcliffe,
G.E.C. Wood, J.W.
Hearne, J.B. Hobbs,
A.E.R. Gilligan,
C. Parkin, P.G.H.
Fender, M.W. Tate,
E.H. Hendren and F.E.
Woolley.
Source: The Hulton
Picture Company

strange if that spirit (Bolshevism), in some shape or form, had not reached the fringes of our first-class cricket grounds.

In a later book, *Cricket Under Fire,* Sewell included photographs he had taken of The Runmaker (Bosser Martin's huge roller at the Oval), Lord Harris playing for Plum Warner's XI against Westminster School at Vincent Square in 1917, and Hobbs leaping out to drive in the nets at the Oval. The book also recycled several pictures from *Cricket Up to Date,* but included some pictures that Sewell had taken in India, where he sold the occasional photograph to the *Times of India.* Perhaps we should not be too critical of the re-use of photographs, for *Cricket Under Fire* was published in 1941, when film was needed for far more important purposes. There was still room for the

artificially posed shot – an outstanding one being that of Warner, H. Lee, J.W. Hearne and N. Haig in what appears to be Sewell's back garden, all dressed to bat, each standing in front of a separate set of stumps, to commemorate 24 May 1920, when all four hit centuries against Sussex at Lord's. The impression given by such a picture is that there was still a degree of novelty about the whole business of visually recording cricket.

Later, Sewell began to use photographs from agencies (notably Sport & General) since they had obtained the best shots of most home Tests, but he clearly thought that there was still room for his own handiwork. The book contains a picture of Sewell in cricket gear but wearing a gas mask, taken in 1916, and an extraordinary one in which he is wearing grey

flannels and golf shoes – 'Included here to show young cricketers an ideal "worst possible" bowling action.' In fact, it's quite good, with a leap not unlike that of Tom Richardson.

Looking at the period leading up to the First World War, with some honourable exceptions in both books and newspapers, most photographic coverage of cricket on the printed page was poor. The *Daily Graphic* and *Daily Mirror,* and the work of Fry and Beldam stood out head and shoulders above the rest. In papers such as the *Daily Express* there were few photographs of cricket, though that journal did manage to include a large photograph of the Stockbrokers' May Day Walk to Brighton. Occasionally, moments of cricket drama were to be found (stumpings, catches, the stroke with which Faulkner completed his century for

MCC against Notts at Lord's on 1 May 1912), but the quality was always poor. The pictures were heavily retouched and of cigarette-card stature. Their interest lies mainly in the way they were framed, often with a triple lined border, and sometimes with an arm or foot extending beyond the border. Clearly more thought was being given to the use of photographs. To this extent the novelty was beginning to wear off and the medium showed signs of maturity. Pictures were now cropped, to make the most effective use of the photograph. The centre of the action could be shown, it was no longer necessary to cover the entire field of play to include a slip catch.

By the time the first-class game returned on a two-day match basis in 1919, however, neither cricket nor photography was the same.

Australia v England, fifth Test match, Sydney, 1925. F.E. Woolley (England) scores a single from the bowling of A.A. Mailey. J.W. Hearne is the non-strike batsman. Photograph: Herbert Fishwick

CHAPTER 5

Coming of Age and Closed Shops 1919-39

*'Photographs have the kind of authority over imagination today,
which the printed word had yesterday, and the spoken word before that.'
– Walter Lippmann, 1922*

THE OUTBREAK of the First World War in August 1914 effectively put an end to first-class cricket for four years. Grace wrote to *The Sportsman* on 27 August 1914 to point out that 'the fighting on the Continent is very severe, and will probably be prolonged. I think the time has come when the county cricket season should be closed, for it is not fitting at a time like this that able-bodied men should be playing day after day and pleasure-seekers look on...' The Oval had already been taken over by the military, many cricketers had enlisted, and the Long Room at Lord's was appropriated by the Army to make hay-nets for their horses. Some cricket survived on both these sites and many others – Sergeant C. Blythe of Kent played for an England Army XI v an Australian Army XI at Lords on 14 July 1917, just four months before he was killed in France – but, if cricket wasn't altogether banned, it was certainly rationed. If the public still wanted cricket photographs, they had to be contented with shots of geese on the square at Lord's, Jessop at a recruiting rally, cricket on the beach at Gallipoli, Trumper's funeral in Sydney, the Old Trafford pavilion being used as a Red Cross hospital and the Dominions team at Lord's.

The War had the opposite effect on photography. The pressure was on the entire industry to improve techniques and equipment and above all to provide better quality results. Though some of the improvements were of little relevance to cricket – aerial photography has limited use in recording anything other than a distant view of a ground, with maybe a queue winding round it – the changes in general provided a peacetime bonus for professional sports photographers once the War was over. In the mid-1920s the Ermanox plate camera and the Leica 35mm camera were developed, compact instruments for which lenses were available that had far greater light-passing power than those of the pre-War years. The blinding flash of magnesium powder was no longer necessary, flashlights were sufficient

Essex v Australians, Leyton, 1930. C.V. Grimmett (1891-1980) bowling. One of Australia's finest leg-break and googly bowlers, he took 100 wickets on each of his three tours to England (1926, 1930, 1934) and later in the season took all ten wickets against Yorkshire. Source: Press Association

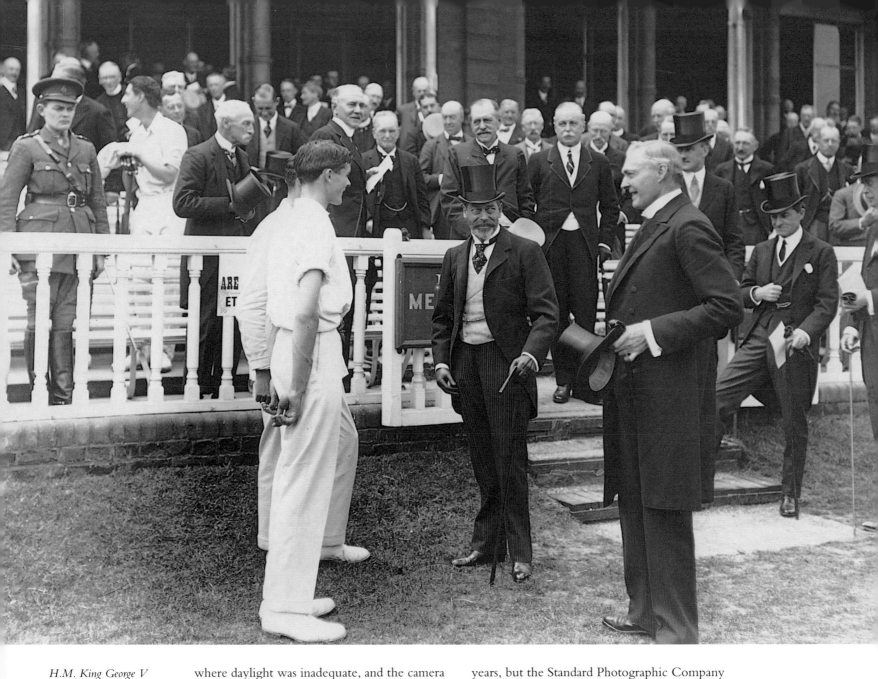

where daylight was inadequate, and the camera could take more candid shots with little or no preparation. This gave a great spurt to photojournalism and the use of photographs in daily and weekly illustrated papers and journals. This, in turn, had a considerable effect on the growth of the photographic agencies. These were by no means new, the first agency specialising in providing pictures for illustration had been formed in 1894: the Illustrated Journals Photographic Supply Company of Ludgate Hill. Like all the early agencies, it was a modest affair – an office, a small darkroom, a typewriter and a camera were all that was needed to be in business. The Illustrated Journals Company lasted only a couple of

years, but the Standard Photographic Company of Bouverie Street, founded in 1895, is still going strong, as the Sport & General Press Agency. Another early agency was Half Tones, set up in Fleet Street in 1906 by two journalists, John Frazer and Michael Roberts. Within a short time, however, Half Tones had been absorbed by the larger agency, Central News.

In the early days it was hard for such agencies to make a living. Pictures were expensive to reproduce, and it took two days to make a block from a negative. As newspapers increased their picture coverage of news and sporting events, however, agencies started to spring up all over the country:

Barratts, Topical, London News Agency, Alfieri's, Central Press Photos and Half Tones. Before the First World War, most newspapers relied entirely on these agencies for their photographic coverage, paying what now seem modest fees for the pictures they used, rather less than one shilling (5p) per square inch. Most newspapers used the agencies, but some – *Daily Mirror, Daily Sketch* and *Daily Graphic* – also had their own staff photographers, or used freelance contributors such as E.H.D. Sewell.

The agencies formed a trade association, the Proprietors Association of Press Photographic Agencies, which closed down in 1933 when some agencies broke ranks on the standard fees charged. The PAPPA was replaced by two organisations, the Photographic News Agencies (made up of London News Agency Photos, Central Press Photos, Fox, Topical, and Sport & General), and the British International

Photographic Press Agencies (Associated Press, Planet, INP, Keystone and Barratts).

The years between the two World Wars were in many ways the golden age of cricket photography. The market for photographs had grown considerably. They were used in newspapers, magazines, pictorial books or cricket programmes, tour and benefit brochures and the dust-jackets of books. The cinema had comparatively little to show in the way of cricket, though the Gaumont British Newsreel Company paid Surrey County Cricket Club £225 for cinematograph rights to the Oval for the 1934 season. The agencies, too, looked for exclusive rights at the key grounds. Central Press paid £100 for exclusive press photographic rights at the same ground in the same year, and similar monopolies were sold at Lord's, Headingley and the other Test match grounds.

Miss Irene Taylor, teacher, cricket and football coach at Gateforth School, Marylebone. The picture is highly posed, and the action highly suspect, but Gateforth School won their junior league.
Source: Hulton Picture Company

There was plenty of opportunity for plenty of photographers. Much of the work of the agencies was extremely good and there were some individually outstanding photographers. One of the greatest was an Australian, Herbert Fishwick, who worked for two New South Wales dailies, the *Sydney Morning Herald* and the *Sydney Mail*. Fishwick was more than a technically good photographer – he had an eye for a picture. His coverage of the 1924-25 Test series in Australia was as comprehensive as it was brilliant, including general views of matches in progress, action shots, portraits of opening pairs walking out to bat, and pictures that captured much of the sweat and tears of the series. There is one lovely photograph of

Maurice Tate bowling near the end of a day's play, with his own shadow splashed across the sun-baked square. Tate bowled 167 eight-ball overs in the first two Tests alone, to take twenty wickets for 469 runs. Australia's bowling hero was Jack Gregory, 'Tall, strong and raw-boned, like one of his native kangaroos', according to the Somerset amateur, R.C. Robertson-Glasgow. In the Test series, Gregory bowled 209 overs and took twenty-two wickets for 816 runs.

Fishwick's most famous shot of all time, however, was taken three years later, during the 1928-29 tour, when MCC played New South Wales. It is the best-ever photograph of Wally Hammond's cover drive. The

The cricket ground Scarborough, September 1921. The last match of the Australian tour of England against Mr C.I. Thornton's XI, and not a bare head in sight.
Source: Press Association

G.N. Francis of the West Indies bowling during the match against Surrey at the Oval, 1923. A.Sandham is the non-strike batsman. Francis (1897-1942) was a right-arm fast bowler who made three tours to England and one to Australia.
Source: Press Association

Australia v England, fourth Test match, Melbourne, 1925. J.M. Gregory of Australia bowling. R. Kilner is the non-strike batsman. Photograph: Herbert Fishwick

M.W. Tate bowling during the MCC tour of Australia 1924-25. His bowling during the five Test matches was an outstanding event of this series. His analysis was 316-62-881-38, and his average 23.18. Photograph: Herbert Fishwick

*Australia v England,
fourth Test match,
Melbourne, 1925.
J.B. Hobbs gives a chance
to C. Kelleway from the
bowling of J.M. Gregory.
H. Sutcliffe is the non-
strike batsman. Hobbs
and Sutcliffe put on 126
for the first wicket and
England defeated
Australia in a Test match
for the first time since
1912.
Photograph: Herbert
Fishwick*

wicketkeeper, Oldfield, has moved across to take the ball should the batsman have missed it, but Hammond has placed his left foot well to the pitch of the ball and there was never any chance that he would have failed to get it in the meat of the bat. A dark handkerchief protrudes from Hammond's right trouser pocket. The left leg is well bent. There is a strong, stocky look to both batsman and bat – Hammond was no wristy Ranji – and we do not see the ball, which was presumably sizzling across the outfield. It is one of the most-reproduced cricket photographs of all time. In the same series, Fishwick caught the dramatic incident when Kippax was controversially given out in the third Test at Adelaide, a decision that could have cost Australia the match. Kippax played at a ball from Tate, missed, and the umpire called 'over'. Duckworth, the wicketkeeper, then pointed to a dislodged bail, lying on the ground. Kippax was convinced that the ball had bounced off

Duckworth's pads and thus dislodged the bail – but he walked.

Fishwick was to some extent lucky in the attitude towards cricket of the papers he worked for. The picture coverage in the *Sydney Mail* was superb, far superior to any contemporary English newspaper. During the Bodyline tour of 1932-33, any single issue might carry as many as twenty large photographs. From the Melbourne Test there were shots of Wall bowling, Sutcliffe cutting, Bradman bowled first ball by Bowes ('note his extraordinary position after making the stroke', ran the caption), Hammond's off-stump somersaulting after being bowled by Wall, and the run-out of O'Brien. The paper was not afraid to devote an entire page to one photograph of O'Reilly's action. The Adelaide Test received even better coverage, with pictures of Woodfull losing his bat while playing Larwood, and Bradman ducking a bouncer ('Whiz! Bradman ducks to safety when

Larwood hurled down a fast flyer'). In none of these marvellous pictures is the photographer credited.

One of the features of cricket photography that the work of Fishwick exemplifies is that, by the 1920s, the camera could not only catch the drama of the game, it could accentuate it. Before the First World War, photographers perched where they could most easily (or hopefully) cover the field of play, often square on to the wicket, at the equivalent of deep extra or deep mid-wicket. Fishwick, and others, realised the importance of choosing the position from which pictures were taken with greater care. By aiming the camera diagonally across the wicket, from the equivalent of deep third man or long-on, Fishwick was able to suggest that a bowler was towering over a batsman, or vice versa. In a series as diplomatically prickly as that of the 1932-33 Bodyline tour, the camera may well have

played its part in inflaming the passions of both sides and the public, with pictures not only of Ponsford, Oldfield and Bradman taking a hammering, but of the full body armour worn by Fingleton and others for self-protection. Certainly, the Woodfull family have their own snapshot of Bill Woodfull staggering away from the wicket after being struck above the heart by a ball from Larwood at Adelaide on 14 January 1933. Even the picture of Jardine leading out the England team at Melbourne in January 1933 has a degree of menace.

By the 1930s, the photo coverage of cricket was all embracing. Every facet of the game could be faithfully recorded, from crowds and players arriving at grounds before the start of play to the celebrations that followed victory or a well-fought draw; from Tests where national pride was at stake to village cricket, where so much more was at stake if Hugh de Selincourt is to be believed. It was also an age when cricket basked in its highest attendances. When Yorkshire and Lancashire, or Surrey and Notts met on a Bank Holiday Saturday, grounds were packed to capacity and beyond. In 1921, 20,000 people a day packed the Oval to see Hitch's benefit game against Sussex. Three years later, on the same ground, 25,000 saw Hobbs hit 105 against Notts and then Fender thrash fifty in half an hour. In some ways this is a chicken-and-egg situation: did cricket become increasingly popular because the camera was regularly recording its finest moments and greatest players, or were photographers present at Lord's, Sydney, Melbourne, Trent Bridge, Headingley, the Wanderers, Sabina Park and the Gymkhana Ground, Bombay simply because cricket was a game with such mass appeal?

The use of the wire photo meant that newspapers in Britain had rapid access to pictures taken on MCC tours abroad. The first regular wire service was in daily use from Marconi House, London, to New York in 1926. Within a short time similar services existed between London and Australia, though

few papers bothered to make use of them during the Bodyline tour. The *Daily Express,* however, did print a photograph of Chapman, Woodfull and Larwood trying to pacify barrackers during the MCC and Victoria match some weeks before trouble flared in the Adelaide Test. The picture was used to illustrate an article by R.W. Thompson, published on the first day of the Adelaide Test, in which he advocated calling off the Test series: 'These "Tests" must stop before more harm is done...'

The camera had also learnt how to act as an eavesdropper, picking up private but significant moments, sometimes catching people off guard. At other times, the photographer's subjects were well aware that they were in the viewfinder, but the pictures that come to us across the years reveal a cricketing age long gone. The photographs taken of the spectators at such games as Eton v Harrow are part of a social archive. The Topical Press photograph of a party arriving at Lord's in 1930 – men in morning suits and top hats, ladies in gowns and broad-brimmed sunhats carrying a large basket

Somerset v Surrey, Taunton, 1925. J.B. Hobbs batting. With scores of 101 in each innings he equalled and then passed the 126 centuries scored by W.G. Grace. The cameras stayed for both innings – not all the crowd did. Source: The Hulton Picture Company

England v Australia, third Test match, Leeds, 1926. J.B.Hobbs and H.Sutcliffe walk out to open for England. In the second innings they scored 156 for the first wicket after England had been forced to follow on. A lovely photograph which was probably taken for mundane purposes – to meet a deadline.
Source: The Hulton Picture Company

RIGHT: *England v Australia, fifth Test match, the Oval, 1926. J.B. Hobbs (100) hits a ball from A.J. Richardson to clear the close-set field during the first wicket partnership, with H. Sutcliffe (161), of 172 in England's second innings. The photograph also includes H. Young (umpire), W.A. Oldfield (wicketkeeper), W.M. Woodfull (extra cover), C.G. Macartney (mid-on) and A.A. Mailey (fine leg).*
Source: Press Association

H. Larwood,
Nottinghamshire and
England. 'I say this
purely and simply as a
bowler judging another –
Larwood was magnificent.'
– Bill Bowes.
Source: The Hulton
Picture Company

A.P.F. Chapman batting during the fifth Test match between England and Australia at the Oval, 1926. He had been appointed captain of England for this Test match in succession to A.W. Carr.
Source: Press Association

of cornflowers, the roads around St John's Wood almost empty of cars – is as much an historical document as Roger Fenton's shot of Hunsdonbury seventy-three years earlier.

It was also the age of a frenzied circulation war between the leading daily papers. As well as vying with each other to provide the best news coverage, special offers or most famous reporters, all the national dailies competed in their sports coverage. The early lead in sports photography of the *Daily Graphic* and *Daily Mirror* had been whittled away by the *Daily Mail* and *Daily Express,* and even *The Times* was beginning to see its back page as more than a gallery for the occasional pretty picture.

There was still a place for the beautiful cricket study, but the public by now expected at least shades of the conflict, images from the battlefield itself. The 1930 Test series between England and Australia was astonishingly well-photographed, as befitted the quality of the players taking part. The Australian batting line-up consisted of Ponsford, Woodfull, Bradman, McCabe and the precocious talents of Archie Jackson. Cardus reckoned the England team of 1930 one of the best ever: Hobbs, Woolley, Hammond, Duleepsinhji, Hendren, Chapman, Allen, Tate, Robins, White and Duckworth. Australia won the series 2-1, with two drawn

The crowds run onto the field at the end of the fifth Test match between England and Australia, the Oval, 1926. England won by 289 runs, the Ashes were regained and they had won a Test series after nearly fourteen years. These scenes were to be repeated in 1953.
Source: The Hulton Picture Company

C.G. Macartney walks into lunch 112 not out (151) during the third Test match between England and Australia, Leeds 1926. He is one of three Australians to score a century before lunch. The others are V.T. Trumper (1902) and D.G. (Sir Donald) Bradman (1930). Source: The Hulton Picture Company

The Eton and Harrow match at Lord's, 1928 – a picture taken more for the society page than the sports page. Source: The Times

games in which the advantage lay with Australia.

Disappointing though much of that year's cricket may have been to England supporters, only the most rabidly chauvinistic of fans could have moaned at the photographs produced that summer, and the summers of 1934 and 1938. Hundreds of wonderful pictures were taken in a decade that began with Hobbs and ended with Hutton, but centred around Bradman. There are plenty of photographs of Grace, and Hobbs, but Bradman was the first cricketer whose entire career has been comprehensively photographed. In the 1930s, he was more than merely the finest batsman in the world, he was a celebrity. Songs were written about him,

gramophone records were made of him playing the piano. For most of his career, 'BRADMAN 0' merited a bigger headline than 'BRADMAN 100'. The English bowlers respected him and the English selectors feared him. He was photographed wherever he went – shopping, the theatre, to Wimbledon, crossing the street, leaving a cricket ground in his white car, chatting with a London policeman. He had film star status. Whether in his whites and baggy cap, or his dark double-breasted suit and snap-brimmed trilby, the smiling superstar from Bowral was one of the most famous figures of the inter-war years.

Where the crowds went, the cameras went too. If a match was poised in an interesting

W.R. Hammond (1903-1965). One of the best-known cricket photographs taken during the match between MCC and New South Wales, November 1928 by Herbert Fishwick. Hammond scored 225. The wicketkeeper is W.A. Oldfield.
Photograph: Herbert Fishwick

position, or if a famous player hovered on the verge of a new record, the cameras stayed overnight, waiting for the next day's excitement. In 1925 agency photographers arrived early at Taunton on the morning of Monday 17 August in expectation of Hobbs equalling Grace's record of 126 first-class centuries. *Wisden* reported that the 'Taunton ground, with its rather short boundaries, might furnish Hobbs with the opportunity he wanted...and a big crowd gathered in the hope of assisting at his triumph.' Hobbs duly obliged, with 101 in the Surrey first innings. Amazingly, though the crowds departed, the cameras stayed for Hobbs's 127th century in the second innings, a feat made possible by the stalwart efforts of Mr J.C.W. MacBryan, Mr J.J. Bridges, Young and Hunt (the last two the only professionals in Somerset's gentlemanly team), who set Surrey a target of 183 to win.

W. Rhodes of Yorkshire bowling in the match against Surrey, the Oval, 1929. He was in his fifty-second year and was to retire the following season (1930).
Source: Press Association

RIGHT: *England v Australia, third Test match, Leeds 1930. D.G. (Sir Donald) Bradman returns through the crowd after scoring 334 – a new Test Match record. A fourteen-year-old Leonard Hutton watched this innings and was to surpass it eight years later.*
Source: The Hulton Picture Company

ABOVE: *England v Australia, second Test match, Lord's, 1930. W.M. Woodfull of Australia offers a chance to W.R. Hammond at slip during his innings of 155. The wicketkeeper is G. Duckworth. Source: Sport & General*

RIGHT: *England v Australia, first Test Match, Trent Bridge, 1930. D.G. (Sir Donald) Bradman batting. His scores were 8 and 131. W.R. Hammond is at gully. F.E. Wooley, slip and G. Duckworth is the wicketkeeper. Source: The Hulton Picture Company*

RIGHT: *England v Australia, fifth Test match, the Oval, 1930. R.E.S. Wyatt batting during his first innings of 64. He had received a death threat after replacing the popular A.P.F. Chapman as England's captain.*
Source: The Hulton Picture Company

RIGHT: *England v Australia, fifth Test match, the Oval, 1930. R.E.S. Wyatt batting during his first innings of 64. He had received a death threat after replacing the popular A.P.F. Chapman as England's captain.*
Source: The Hulton Picture Company

BELOW: *Essex v Yorkshire, Leyton, 1932. H. Sutcliffe (313) batting during the record first-wicket partnership in England with P. Holmes (224) of 555. This passed by one run the previous record also by a Yorkshire opening partnership, J.T. Brown and J. Tunnicliffe in 1898.*
Source: The Hulton Picture Company

G.O. Allen (Sir George) (1902-89) bowling at the Oval, 1932. A typical agency shot.
Source: Press Association

Australia v England, second Test match, Melbourne, 1933. D.R. Jardine, captain of England, leads the team into the field. Left to right: H. Sutcliffe, W.E. Bowes, L.E.G. Ames, D.R. Jardine, R.E.S. Wyatt and W. Voce.
Source: The Hulton Picture Company

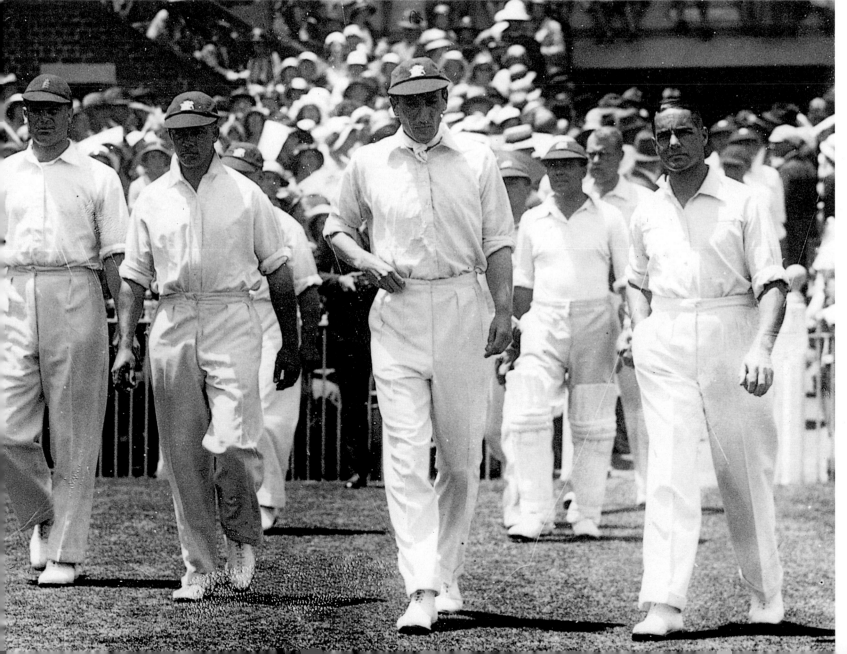

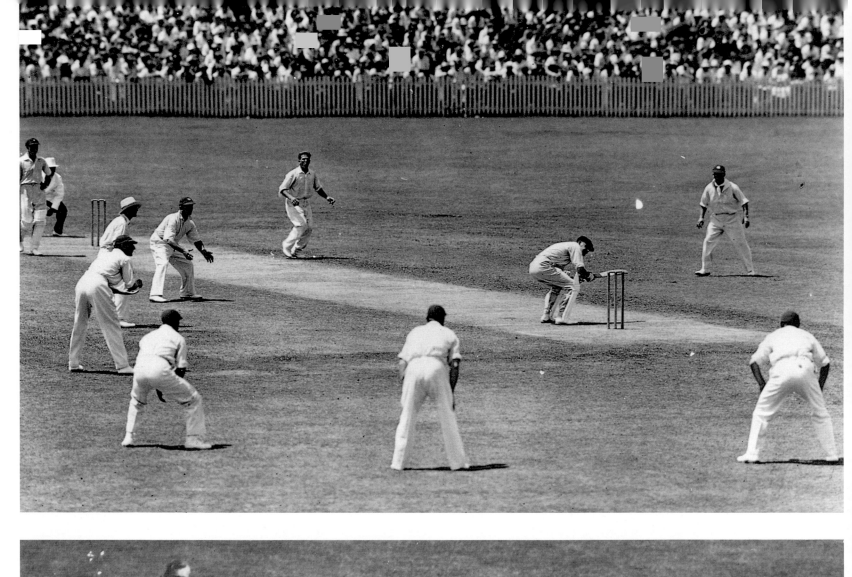

Nottinghamshire v Australia, Trent Bridge, 1934. W. Voce bowling to W.M. Woodfull with a leg theory field set. There was a protest from the Australians and Voce was absent on the last day of play with a 'leg injury'.

ABOVE LEFT: *Australia v England, fourth Test match, Brisbane, 1933. W.M. Woodfull of Australia ducks to a bouncer from H. Larwood. Source: The Hulton Picture Company*

BELOW LEFT: *Australia v England, second Test match, Melbourne, 1932-33. D.G. (Sir Donald) Bradman bowled by W.E. Bowes, first ball, for a duck. Bradman scored 103 not out in Australia's second innings. Source: The Hulton Picture Company*

The Aldershot cricket ground, 1934, during the match between the Army and the Australians. Source: The Hulton Picture Company

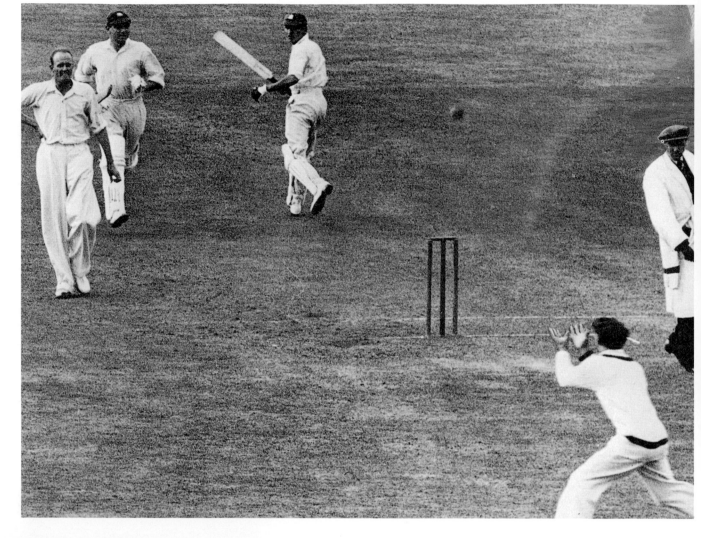

As for the glass raised by Hobbs while at the wicket, not even the camera can tell us whether it was champagne or orange juice.

Matters were easier all round at Leyton in 1932, when Holmes and Sutcliffe established a new world record partnership for the first wicket. By Wednesday night they had already put on well over 400 runs. Photographers gathered on Thursday morning to cover whatever happened, and have left us a fine collection of Holmes batting, Sutcliffe batting, Sutcliffe's eventual dismissal (bowled by Eastman), and the Yorkshire pair standing proudly in front of the tiny scoreboard, already almost a photographic cliché in cricket terms.

Professional photographers from the agencies gathered for every Test without the need for a promise of excitement to come. They were at

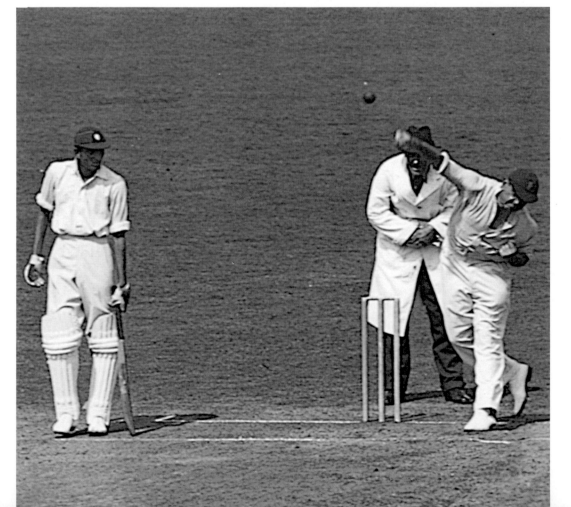

England v India, third Test match, the Oval, 1936. W.R. Hammond batting during his innings of 217.
Source: The Hulton Picture Company

England v India, third Test match, the Oval, 1936. W.R.Hammond bowling. 'Had the gods denied him batting talent, he could have found fame as a bowler.'
– J.M. Kilburn.
Source: The Hulton Picture Company

England v New Zealand, third Test match, the Oval, 1937. D.C.S. Compton batting during his innings of 65. This was Compton's first Test appearance for England. Source: The Hulton Picture Company

D.G. (Sir Donald) Bradman and W.R.Hammond (1903-65), captains of Australia and England during the Test series of 1938. The sartorial detail of the raincoats is magnificent. Source: The Hulton Picture Company

Headingley in July 1926 to see Macartney get a century before lunch, after he'd been dropped fourth ball by the England captain, A.W. Carr. The resulting shot of Macartney returning to the pavilion, 112 not out, doffing his cap to the Yorkshire crowd, is a fine record of a wonderful moment. Complementary to it is the photograph taken a couple of days later, of Hobbs and Sutcliffe walking out to lead England's fight back. We now know that they put on 156 together for England's first wicket, and we have to take care not to read too much into such a photograph in the light of that

knowledge. But the picture has its own bursting power and emotion, pride and hope, one of the best pictures of The Old Firm ever taken.

Sadly, there were the ones that seem to have got away. No camera was at Headingley on 12 July 1932, when Hedley Verity took 10 for 10 against Notts. It may be that the photographers had all gone home, for at lunch Notts were 38 for 0 and clearly playing for a draw. In just over an hour after lunch, Verity ran through the card, taking ten wickets while the batsmen scored seven runs off him.

England v Australia, fifth Test match, the Oval, 1938. L. Hutton (Sir Leonard) batting during his innings of 364 – an innings recorded in detail by the agency photographers. Source: The Hulton Picture Company

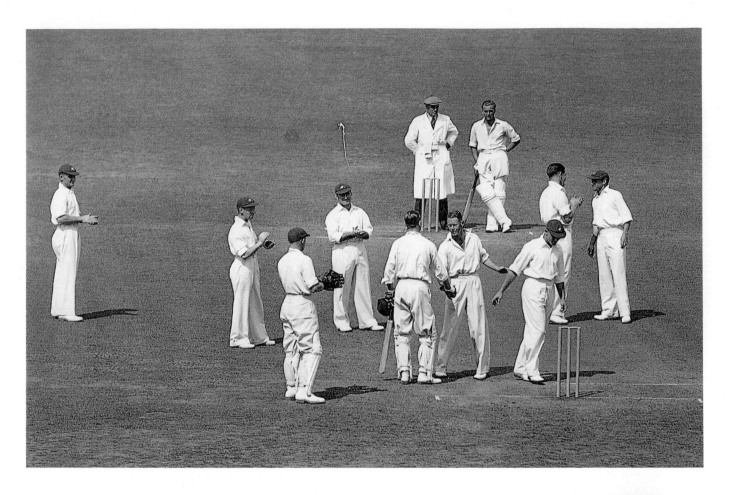

LEFT: *Hutton shakes hands with W.A. Brown after passing Bradman's score of 334 made in 1930.*
Source: *The Hulton Picture Company*

RIGHT: *Hutton returns to the pavilion at the end of his innings which lasted for over thirteen hours.*
Source: *The Hulton Picture Company*

Listening to the radio while queuing to enter the Oval – time passed slowly inside and outside the ground.
Source: The Hulton Picture Company

Home Counties v The Rest of England, at Northampton, 1938. P. Snook ct. M. Kynvin b. M. Maclagan 1 (first innings). The first recorded women's cricket match was in 1745 between Bramley and Hambleton. It was played on Gosden Common near Guildford. Women made their first appearance at Lord's in 1976 in a match between England and Australia.
Source: The Hulton Picture Company

*D.G. (Sir Donald)
Bradman on the golf
course, 1934.
Source: The Hulton
Picture Company*

*A sequence of photographs
taken in 1939 showing
the bowling action of
H. Verity (1905-1943)
using the 'Magic Eye'
camera of Fox Photos.
Source: The Hulton
Picture Company*

England v West Indies,
second Test match, Old
Trafford, 1939.
G.A. Headley (1909-
83) batting. He made
scores of 51 and 5.
A. Wood is the
wicketkeeper.
'All you have to do is to
get there in time and then
whatever the pace of the
bowling you use the left
wrist and left hand and
you can put the ball
wherever you please.'
– G.A. Headley.
Source: The Hulton
Picture Company

Photographed by Bert Hardy of Picture Post *outside the Grace Gates, Lord's 1939. Peter Wagner (left) and 'Timmy' Ryson (centre) are from Harrow School. The group of three boys on the right are (left to right) George Salmon, Jack Catlin and George Young. One of* Picture Post's *political photographs. Source: The Hulton Picture Company*

Middlesex v Yorkshire, Lord's 1939. Rev E.T. Killick of Middlesex is caught by A. Mitchell off the bowling of H. Verity for 6 (first innings). Source: Sport & General

L.N. Constantine (Lord) (1901-71) of West Indies bowling during the match against Essex at Leyton in 1939. Source: The Hulton Picture Company

CHAPTER 6

The Age
of the
Agency

'The Golden Rule is "keep your eye off the ball".'
— Steve Powell and Tony Duffy, 1984

IN SOME WAYS, the high-water mark of pre-War cricket photography was the timeless Test at the Oval in August 1938. Although the photography was all in the hands of one agency, the Central Press, the visual coverage of that Test was all-embracing, from the first day picture of Hammond and Bradman, flanking the chief groundsman, the immense Bosser Martin, to the shot of Fleetwood-Smith and Hutton grabbing souvenir stumps five days later, almost every detail was recorded. There were those who cautioned against a timeless Test, and the *Daily Mail*'s prognosis on the first day warned of what was to come: 'Long-nursed by "Bosser" Martin, the Test wicket at Kennington Oval now wears that smooth, concrete-like surface...offering no grip to the ball...' Cardus wondered how many of the Chelsea pensioners watching would live to see the end of the game. Woodfull asked about the possible effects of snow on the wicket. Tom Webster, in his cartoon, expected a result some time in November.

But by the end of the first day, public, papers and press photographers were hooked. Not only were there plenty of pictures of the first day's play, when Hutton and Leyland put on 300 after Edrich had been lbw to O'Reilly for twelve, but the heroes were pursued throughout the next twenty-four hours, which was Sunday and a rest day. There were pictures of Verity and Hutton playing cricket on the beach at Bognor, of Leyland playing golf at Woodcote Park, Epsom. On Monday morning, cameras were ready to record Hutton leaving his hotel with Hardstaff. Meantime, the agencies had searched through their files and found a variety of background photographs of Hutton – for it seemed that a new record might well be in the air. There were pictures of Pudsey and of Hutton with his cricketing brothers, Edmund, George and Reginald, courtesy of the *Telegraph and Argus*.

On that Monday, Hutton stayed at the crease all day, with Leyland for a while, Hammond for longer, Paynter and Compton

E.R. Dexter batting to the bowling of W.W. Hall in the third Test match between England and the West Indies in Jamaica, 1960. The ball appears stuck to the bat – an example of the occasional freak photograph.

An England XI v West Indies, Lord's, 1944. L.N. Constantine, captain of the West Indies XI, leads the team onto the field.
Source: Sport & General

briefly, and then endlessly with Hardstaff. Cardus fumed at the way Hardstaff played a string of half-volleys gently back to the bowler with the score at some 700 for 5: 'The Australians stuck to the hopeless toil philosophically and Bradman changed his bowling, and the umpires counted the overs, and the runs mounted, and the clouds rolled on, and the gas-holder went up and down, and the trams went by the ground, and the hours waxed and waned, and somewhere even the dreariest river wound safe to sea.' Another fifty words that did little to describe the state of play; the camera was driving Cardus further and further away from writing about cricket. For, he might have added, the cameras clicked, inside and outside the ground. There were already those who sought to obtain pirate photographs from roofs and upper windows of the flats surrounding the Oval, recalling the advice of the *British Journal of Photography* way back in 1912 – 'Get pictures by legitimate means if possible, but get pictures'.

And so we have pictures of the queues outside the ground, in trilbies and creased raincoats, listening to gramophones or portable wireless sets; of Hutton raising his three hundred; of Hutton passing Hammond and Bradman's previous record highest scores in Test cricket; of Bradman congratulating him (Central Press); of the scoreboard registering the new record; of the crowd rising to acknowledge thirteen hours' concentration; of Hutton triumphant and weary, returning to the pavilion (Fox Photos); of Bradman being carried from the field, smiling (or is it grimacing?) with a twisted ankle; and of down to and beyond the last rites.

It was perhaps as well that such riches were on offer. Just over a year later, the Second World War began, first-class cricket disappeared, and cricket photography was confined to the occasional group of khaki clad heroes, or the game persisting in some lovely hamlet despite the worst efforts of Hitler, or of some of the oddities of war, such as the shot of players flinging themselves to the ground at Lord's while a flying bomb passes overhead. Many of these photographs have an almost unbearable poignancy – such as that of Verity's father talking with his son and Kenneth Farnes in 1939; both Verity and Farnes were killed during the War.

As in the First World War, much was done

to improve photographic equipment, and there was a shortage of film for non-essential purposes. It is significant that Eric Midwinter's excellent book on *The Lost Seasons – 1939-1945* contains no photographs. Nor was it even a time for lavish reproductions of earlier photographic masterpieces: throughout the War there were strict controls on the amount and quality of paper used for text in books, let alone photographs. And the pictures that the newspapers wished to print were of more bellicose matters.

Towards the end, the powers-that-be relented a little. The agencies maintained their respective (if not respected) monopolies, and so Sport & General returned to Headquarters for their pictures of the Victory Matches at Lord's, when Pilot Officer K.R. Miller belted his way to prominence, under the gaze of Field Marshal Montgomery, newly returned from Luneberg Heath, and when, uncharacteristically, 'Australia did not reach England's standard of high-class fielding' (*Wisden*).

Though it took a while for papers and magazines to get back to a pre-War 'normal',

in terms of the popularity of cricket, it was business as usual, with crowds flocking back to the grounds (the gates had to be shut at the Oval in 1948 during a match between Surrey and Glamorgan!), and new heroes to be photographed. In 1946 Alec Bedser made his Test debut and had immediate success. The following year belonged to Edrich and Compton, as they broke one record after another. Compton's role in the history of cricket photography is perhaps unique – the first English cricketing superstar with added glamour. Like Bradman, he was followed and photographed wherever he went. Unlike Bradman, he was also wanted for his good looks. He appeared, clad in dinner jacket, in advertisements for Brylcream, reputedly earning vast sums of money for doing so. There were those who choked with rage and swore it brought the game into disrepute, but, for hundreds of thousands of schoolboys, Compton was an idol. As with Humphrey Bogart and James Cagney, the camera was kind to Compton, even when it caught him dragging on a cigarette while he buckled on his pads.

K.R. Miller of Australia batting during the Victory Test matches between England and Australia in 1945. In the five matches he scored 443 runs which included two centuries at Lord's.
Source: Sport & General

England v India, third Test match, the Oval, 1946. V.M. Merchant of India batting during his innings of 128. W.R. Hammond is at slip and T.G. Evans is the wicketkeeper. Source: The Hulton Picture Company

Surrey v India, the Oval, 1946. The photograph was taken during the tenth-wicket stand of 249 between C.T. Sarwate (124 not out) and S. Bannerjee (121). Source: The Hulton Picture Company

The following year, ten years after the débâcle at the Oval, the Australians returned with what many regard as the finest team ever. They were impressively powerful and awesomely reliable, whether batting or in the field. They won their first eight matches on the trot, seven of them by an innings, the largest victory being over Essex by an innings and 451 runs. The match was played at Southend, and, quite by chance, Carl Sutton, one of the staff photographers with the *Picture Post* was there. He had with him a specially adapted cine camera, with a slow wind, that could take action sequences of a bowler's action, or any particular stroke of a batsman – it took about eight frames to cover delivery or each stroke. That day Australia scored 721 runs (Bradman 187, Brown 153, Loxton 120, Saggers 104 not

out), and Sutton took over 2000 photographs. A tiny number were used in a *Picture Post* spread, but ninety-nine per cent of them remain – unseen, unprinted negatives – in the Hulton Deutsch Picture Library. *Picture Post* is not remembered for its sports coverage, but Bert Hardy and company covered many aspects of cricket.

When the Australians next visited Britain, in 1953, it was for what came to be known as the Coronation Tests, although the first Test began nine days after the Coronation itself. It is now generally accepted that 2 June 1953 saw the birth of mass-audience television. From then on, life was never the same for the cinema, radio or, indeed, commercial photography. Television cameras were at the Oval in August, giving special coverage of the last couple of hours play, when England regained the Ashes. Over the next twenty years, more and more cricket was televised – Tests, one-day internationals, the Gillette Cup, even the occasional three-day county match. The viewer at home could now see cricket action as never before, and, once video recording was in use, he or she could see it over and over again, at normal speed or in slow motion. In the 1950s and 1960s, this may have had little effect on still cricket photography, but, over the years, it has meant that any cricket photograph that is to catch and hold the attention has to be technically of the highest standard, be timed to perfection, and have some dramatic quality. In a hundred years time the modern photograph will have an historical signicance, but not today. It isn't enough to have taken a picture of Gooch or Tendulkar or Dean Jones. It isn't

enough to have taken a good action picture of Waqar Younis, Malcolm Marshall or Imran Khan. Television has given us a surfeit of visual images, covering every piece of the action, often from several angles. The great cricket photograph now has to capture not only the moment, the action, the drama: it has to illuminate what happened and enable us to come to some understanding of the people taking part.

One of the early effects of televising cricket was an increased market for picture souvenirs of summers, series and celebrities. In 1953 the Hulton Press published the *Picture Post Book of the Tests,* with a text by Denzil Batchelor. The highlights of each Test were covered on a day by day basis, so that photographs of the Lord's Test included Hutton batting almost one-handed (he had injured his left hand while fielding), Benaud aggressively fielding to his own bowling, the three England wickets falling on the evening of the fourth day (Hutton, Kenyon and Graveney), and the heroes of the last day's play – Watson and Bailey. The book was published in the autumn of that year, but was more successful than a follow-up a year later.

The pictures for such books still came from the agencies, whose monopoly continued until 1972. There is some dispute as to how and why the monopoly eventually came to an end. Certainly, the early 1970s were times of considerable change in the sporting world. The 1969-70 Springbok rugby tour of Britain was constantly interrupted with scenes of protest and violence. In May 1970 the Cricket Council withdrew its invitation to the South African cricketers. Six months later, the Australian Board of Control withdrew a similar invitation to the Springboks to tour Australia. 1972 was another Ashes year, an exciting shared rubber, with Australia winning the final Test at the Oval by five wickets thanks to centuries by the Chappell brothers. The Australians played some part in the collapse of the agency monopoly, for they had announced that they were bringing their own photographer with them to

D.C.S. Compton (right) (110) and W.J. Edrich (106) walking out to bat for Middlesex v Sussex at Lord's in 1947 – a year when they spent much cricketing time together. Source: Sport & General

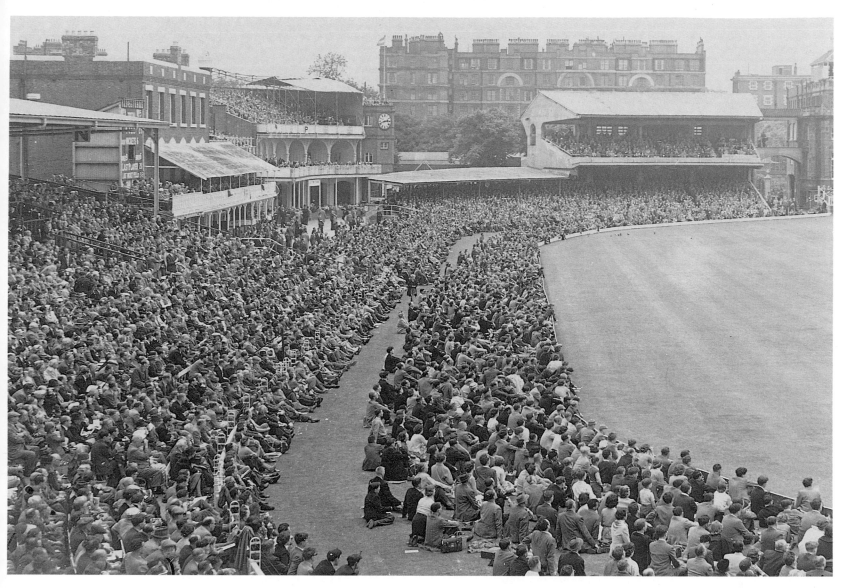

cover the tour. Patrick Eagar and others had been chipping away at the agency stranglehold, supported by writers such as E.W. Swanton. At the same time, many Fleet Street papers had decided that enough was enough and they wanted to use their own photographers to cover cricket. The monopolies enjoyed at Twickenham and other sporting venues had come to an end – now it was cricket's turn. The effect of the end of the monopoly was immediate: most cricket books publishing photographs of the 1972 Tests credit individual photographers rather than agencies. Some of the fine adjustment, however, took a little while – even in 1972 one of the Test match grounds issued passes to photographers with the words 'photography strictly forbidden' stamped across the bottom.

Until the 1970s, most of the cameras used to take pictures of cricket were still of the Long Tom or Long Jimmy variety. These were the names given to the lenses, housing and camera, most of which were home-made and all of which really were long. The first equipment used by Ken Kelly at Headingley in 1938, when he was a photographic assistant on the *Yorkshire Evening News* had a 40-inch-long Dallmeyer lens. In most cases, the lenses were still those that had been made originally for aerial photography from balloons, many of them made in Germany by Zeiss and others, some reputedly recovered from the wreckage

Full house at Lord's. The occasion is the second Test match between England and Australia, 1956. The well-ordered crowd sits on the grass, with not an advertising hoarding in sight.
Source: Sport & General

of zeppelins that had been shot down during the First World War. The drawbacks of such equipment were many. It was hard but essential to focus accurately, the camera had to be held rigidly steady, and the plates for the cameras were bulky, heavy and expensive. They were also rationed. A photographer would be lucky if he was given fifty plates to cover a whole day's cricket, so he had to choose what he shot with great care, and his timing had to be impeccable.

In *An Eye for Cricket,* Patrick Eagar tells the story of one of the most famous cricket photographs of all time. 'The old camera was still in use in 1960–61 when Australia played West Indies at Brisbane. The excitement of the closing overs meant that those photographers who were still on the ground had used up nearly all their allocation. As the match drew to a climax, shortage of plates became a major problem...in the final over, when all four results

were still possible, only Ron Lovitt of *The Age* and Harry Martin of the *Sydney Morning Herald* were still photographing. They realised that any action would happen very quickly, probably more quickly than they could change over plates. They came to an agreement: Martin would photograph the stroke no matter what happened. He would therefore be looking for the winning run, or would photograph Kline, the last batsman, being clean bowled or lbw. Lovitt, positioned alongside, and to Martin's right, would take the action following the stroke – a catch, a run out or a victory salute...Hall bowled to Kline, who pushed the ball away on the leg side – Martin took his photograph as planned. Solomon swooped in and threw the wicket down. Lovitt waited that fraction of a second, the mark of a good photographer. The action developed as Kanhai leapt in the air. That was the moment...Martin, meanwhile, had reloaded his camera and, as some consolation prize, took the players leaving the field.'

Seven years later, in 1968, Dennis Oulds was still using a Long Tom camera at the Oval on the extraordinary last day's play. Here he took a wonderful series of pictures, some of the best and most reproduced cricket photographs. Rain brought the players in to lunch a minute early and a freak thunderstorm flooded the ground. For three hours Ted Warn (the Oval groundsman), his staff, and members of the public fought with mops, sponges and poles (tapping the Oval's drainage system) to get rid of the sheet of water. At a quarter-to-five the match resumed, with Australia needing an impossible 267 runs to win, and needing to hold out for seventy-five minutes to save the game and win the series, with five wickets in hand. The sixth wicket fell with just over thirty-five minutes play left. Cowdrey brought back Underwood from the pavilion end. Oulds was confronted with the rare spectacle of all thirteen players in frame, as England clustered nearer and nearer to the bat. In four-and-a-half overs, Underwood took the last four wickets, and England won with six minutes to spare when Brown snatched up a catch almost off the face of McKenzie's bat.

For some, this is one of the best-ever cricket pictures. Vic Fowler, another agency photographer, regards it as his favourite, a picture he would dearly loved to have taken. Circumstances, the state of the game, dictated that it was there for the taking; the skill and the experience of the photographer made sure it was taken. There may well have been a licking of lips in the photographers' perch at the Oval that afternoon.

England v Australia, fourth Test match, Leeds, 1948. R.N. Harvey of Australia batting. He scored 112 and 4 not out. Harvey, aged nineteen, was playing in his first Test match against England.
Source: Sport & General

England v Australia, first Test match, Trent Bridge, 1948. J. Hardstaff ct. K.R. Miller b. W.A. Johnstone 0.
Source: The Hulton Picture Company

Within the restrictions imposed by grounds on which they worked, agency photographers produced great results. What was wrong with the monopoly system was not that it failed to deliver the goods, but that it held back the growth of cricket photography as a profession, as a way of life, and as a developing art and craft. The death of the monopoly was timely – it could hardly have co-existed with the growth of sponsorship in the game.

But, while it lasted, the agency stranglehold had two great achievements: it gave comprehensive day-by-day coverage of most important matches, and it ensured that libraries were created where the negatives were preserved. The fact that we still draw so heavily on these collections is some kind of tribute to the system.

'The Crowd Within and
the Crowd Without' was
the title of Jack Hickes'
award-winning
photograph taken at
Headingley, Leeds, in
1948.
Source: Jack Hickes
Photographers Limited

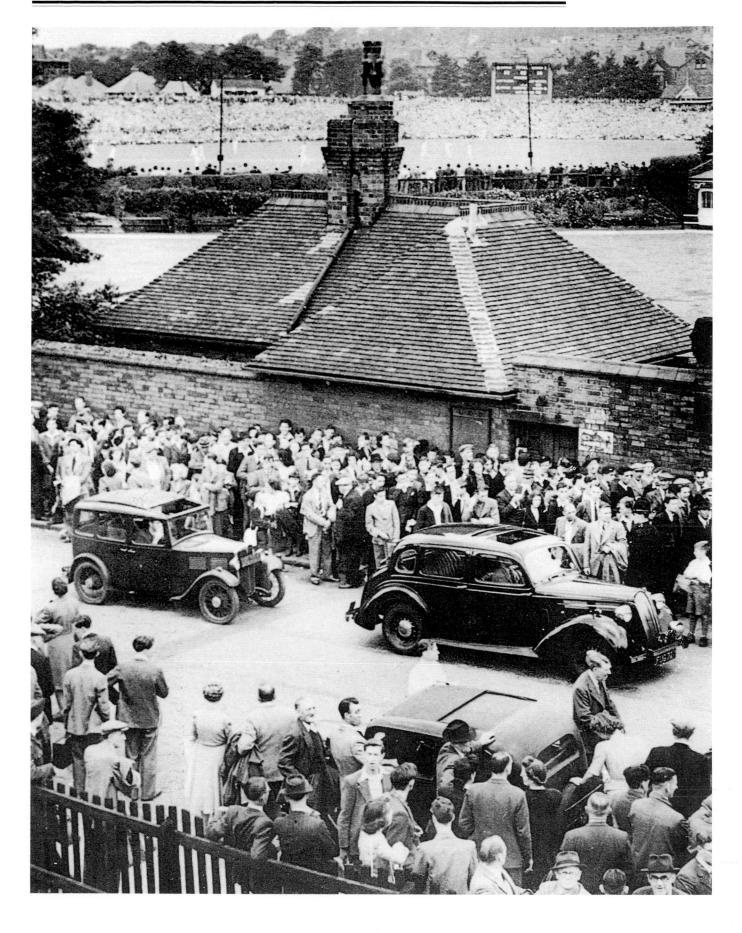

*Women's Cricket
Association v The Rest,
the Oval, 1954.
Miss J. Ellidge at slip fails
to catch Miss S.M. Pilling
(W.C.A.) from the
bowling of Miss S. Brown.
It is interesting to contrast
the definition of this picture
with that of the Home
Counties game in 1938
(page 93).
Source: The Hulton
Picture Company*

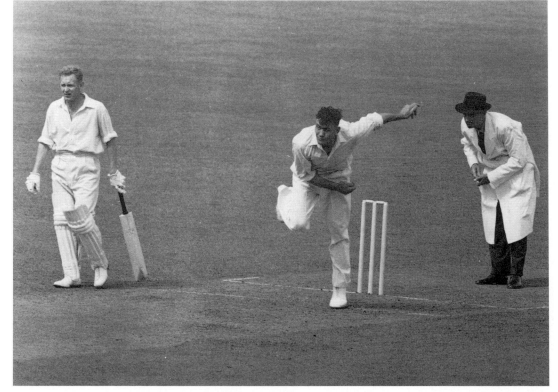

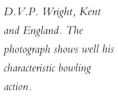

D.V.P. Wright, Kent and England. The photograph shows well his characteristic bowling action.
Source: The Hulton Picture Company

'The Compton Sweep'. D.C.S. Compton batting for the MCC v New Zealand, Lord's 1949 He scored 63. The wicketkeeper is F.L.H. Mooney.
Source: Sport & General

The three Ws – F.M.M. (Sir Frank) Worell, C.L. Walcott and E.deC. Weekes. They were photographed together in recognition of their achievements on the 1950 tour of England. Photograph: Roger Woods

Two photographers from The Times *covering the fifth Test match between England and South Africa, the Oval, 1951. Source: The Times*

Camouflage nets at the Oval put up by the photographic agency holding the rights to photography on the ground to prevent other photographers/agencies from taking photographs, 1956. Source: The Times

A cricket match at the Millbrook Recreation Ground, Southampton, 1950. In the background is RMS Queen Elizabeth I in the King George V drydock for her annual overhaul.
Source: Press Association

F.R.Brown (1910-91) captain of the MCC team to Australia 1950-51 leads them into the field for the match against South Australian Country XI at Renmark.
Source: The Hulton Picture Company

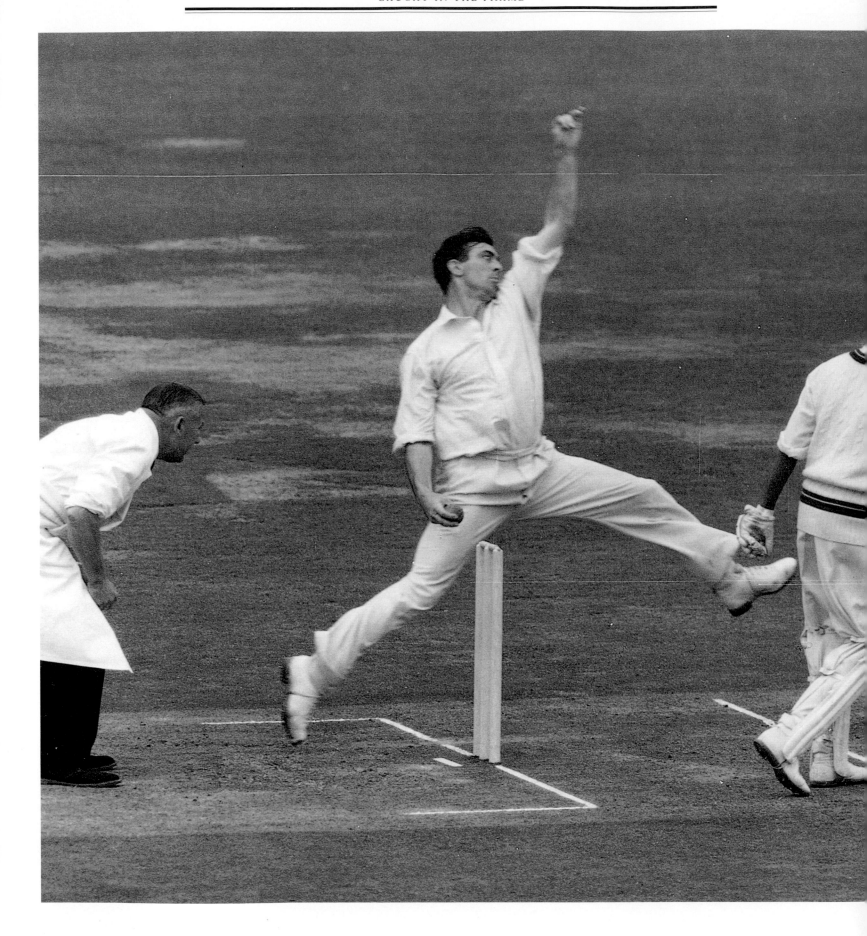

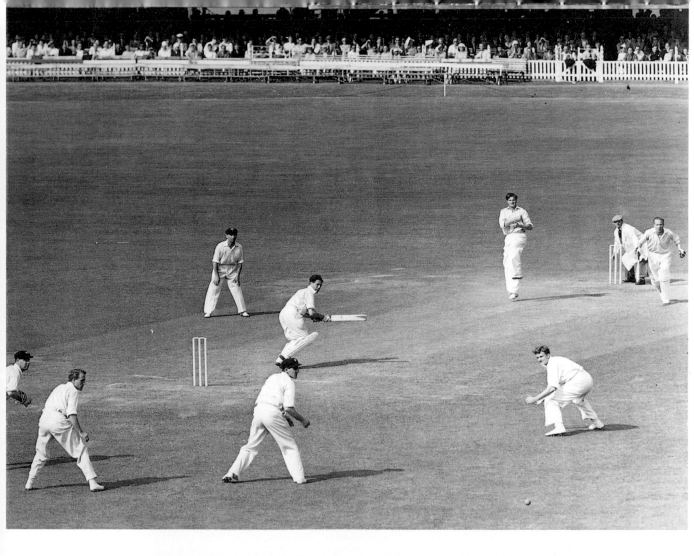

England v Australia, second Test match, Lord's 1953. The stand between T.E. Bailey (71) and W. Watson (109) in England's second innings saved the match for them. The stand lasted from 12.40 to 5.50 pm. Bailey is seen cutting K.R. Miller to third man. The fielders are A.L. Hassett, G.R. Langley, wicketkeeper, G.B. Hole, A.K. Davidson, and R. Benaud. H.G. Baldwin is the umpire. Source: Sport & General

RIGHT: *England v Australia, fifth Test match, the Oval, 1953. D.C.S. Compton and W.J. Edrich running through the crowds after England had won the game by eight wickets and regained The Ashes after twenty years. Source: The Hulton Picture Company*

LEFT: *F.S. Trueman, Yorkshire and England. 'He was no Greek statue, but the truncated breadth of his characteristically square fast-bowler's frame was lined with an even strength from shoulder to hip.' – Frank Tyson. Source: Sport & General*

England v Australia, fifth Test match, the Oval, 1953. R.R. Lindwall was Australia's outstanding fast bowler in the years following the Second World War. He and K.R. Miller proved a formidable fast bowling partnership.
Source: The Hulton Picture Company

England v Australia, third Test match, Leeds, 1956. C.C.McDonald ct. T.G. Evans b. F.S.Trueman 2 (first innings).
Source: Sport & General

RIGHT: *F. Tyson bowling in Australia in 1954-55 when he took the Australians by surprise. A photograph by Willie Vanderson of Fox Photos.*
Source: The Hulton Picture Company

England v Australia, fourth Test match, Old Trafford, 1956. L. Maddocks lbw. b. J.C.Laker 2 (second innings). This was Laker's tenth wicket of the innings and his nineteenth for the match. Left to right (rear): M.C. Cowdrey, L. Maddocks, T.G. Evans, G.A.R. Lock, Rev. D.S. Sheppard, A.S.M. Oakman. Left to right (front): I.W. Johnson, non-strike batsman, F.S. Lee, umpire, J.C. Laker. Source: Sport & General

England v Australia, fourth Test match, Old Trafford, 1956. J.C. Laker leaves the field at the end of the match with figures of 9-37 and 10-53. This was the second time that he had taken all 10 wickets against the Australians. For Surrey he took 10-88. Left to right: P.E. Richardson, A.S.M. Oakman, P.B.H.May, Rev. D.S. Sheppard, J.C. Laker, J.B. Statham. This Test match was covered by three photographers from Sport & General: Bill Bishop, Ken Saunders and Brian Thomas. Source: Sport & General

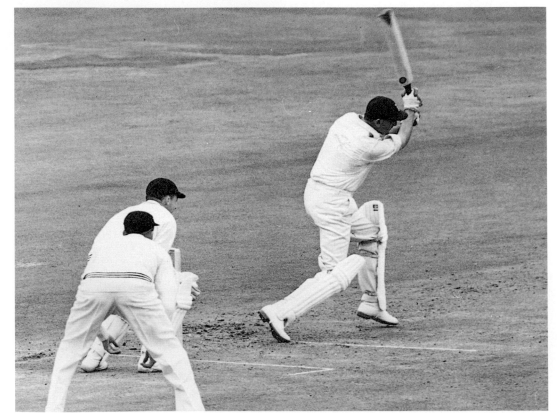

MCC v South African XI, Pretoria, 1956. B. Taylor was lbw b. H. Tayfield in both innings. The South African XI won by 38 runs. This was the first time that MCC had lost a match in South Africa on a turf pitch; their first defeat since 1930-31 and their first defeat outside a Test match since 1913-14.
Source: The Hulton Picture Company

Shades of Herbert Fishwick. T.W. Graveney batting during the second Test match between England and New Zealand at Lord's in 1958.
Source: Sport & General

Old Test Players
taken at Lords June 1957.

Back Row: G. Duckworth, L. E. S. Ames, A. E. R. Gilligan, N. E. Haig, R. E. S. Wyatt, Ian Peebles, E. Clarke.
(Lancs) (Kent) (Sussex) (Middlesex) (Warwick & Worcs) (Middlesex) (N'hants)

Front Row: Geo. Gunn, F. E. Woolley, Robt. Menzies, Sir Pelham Warner, W. Rhodes, S. F. Barnes, P. Mead
(Notts) (Kent) (P.M. Australia) (Middlesex) (Yorks) (Lancs & Staffs) (Hants)

R.G. Menzies (Sir Robert
1894-1978) Prime
Minister of Australia with
a group of former England
Test match players, Lord's
1957. The caption to this
photograph was written by
S.F. Barnes (1873-1967).
Source: Sport & General/
Marylebone Cricket Club

*Australia v West Indies,
first Test match,
Brisbane, 1960. The
dramatic end to the first
'tied' Test in cricket
history. With the scores
equal L. Meckiff is run
out by J. Solomon. This
photograph was taken by
Ron Lovitt.
Source: The Hulton
Picture Company*

G. Griffin of South
Africa bowling during the
second Test match against
England at Lord's,
1960. He was no-balled
eleven times during the
England innings and a
further four times during
an exhibition match
which followed, due to his
bowling action. He also
became the first South
African to achieve a hat-
trick in a Test match.
Source: Sport & General

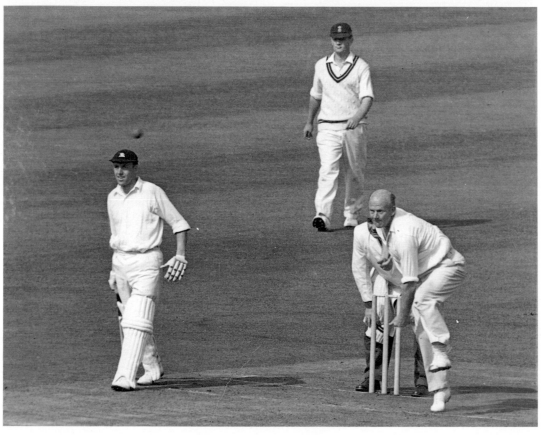

G.A.R. Lock bowling
during the Middlesex v
Surrey game at Lord's in
1962. D.A.D. Sydenham
is the fielder and J.T.
Murray is the non-strike
batsman.
Source: Sport & General

C.C. Griffith bowling
during the fourth Test
match between England
and West Indies, Leeds,
1963. There were
occasions when Griffith's
boots had to be cut from
his swollen feet at the end
of a day's play.
Source: Sport & General

M.C. Cowdrey reaches his century (119) in the second Test match between England and New Zealand at Lord's, 1965. B.R. Taylor is at slip and the wicketkeeper is A.E.Dick.
Source: Sport & General

K.F. Barrington (1930-81) batting during the first Test match between England and South Africa, Lord's, 1965. He scored 91 in the first innings. J.D. Lindsay is wicketkeeper and this game was the 100th Test match between the two countries.
Source: Sport & General

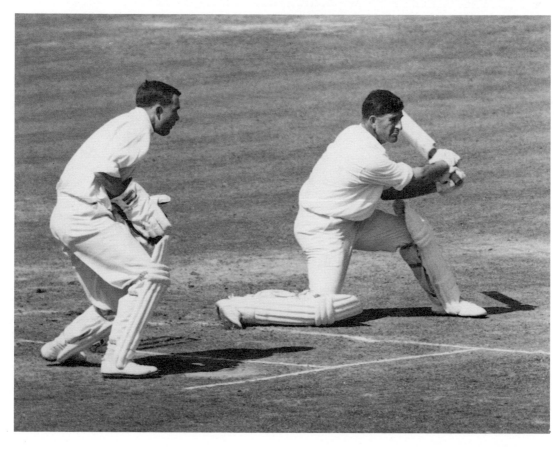

*England v West Indies,
first Test match, Old
Trafford, 1966. W.E.
Russell ct. G.St.A. Sobers
b. L.R. Gibbs 26 (first
innings).
Source: The Hulton
Picture Company*

Australia v England,
third Test match, Sydney,
1966. D.J. Sincock ct.
M.J.K. Smith b. D.A.
Allen 27 (second
innings). The photograph
was taken with a 400mm
lens and 2x tele-converter
which the photographer
had just bought in Japan.
Photograph: Ken Kelly

Kent v Gloucestershire,
Dartford, 1967. A
quarter of a century later,
the photograph has become
an historical document,
full of nostalgic detail.
Source: The Times

C. Milburn batting during the second Test match at Lord's between England and Australia, 1968. He scored 83 and this was the 200th Test match between the two countries.
Source: Sport & General

England v West Indies, second Test match, Lord's, 1969. G.St.A. Sobers is run out in the first innings by G. Boycott for 29. The agony of the other batsman C.A. Davis is only too evident!
Source: Sport & General

England v Australia, fifth Test match, the Oval, 1968. One of several photographs taken by Dennis Oulds of Central Press showing the whole of the England team crowded around the wicket. The only person missing is the square leg umpire. G.D. Mckenzie ct. D.J. Brown b. D.L. Underwood 0 (second innings).
Source: The Hulton Picture Company

England v The Rest of the World XI, fourth Test match, Leeds, 1970. D. Wilson is caught by M.J. Denness (substitute) off the bowling of E.J. Barlow. This was the third wicket of a hat-trick. Barlow had now taken 4 wickets in 5 balls. In the five Test matches he scored 353 runs, took 20 wickets and held 10 catches.
Source: Sport & General

CHAPTER 7

The Modern Age

'The camera makes everyone a tourist in other
people's reality, and eventually in one's own'
— Susan Sontag, 1974

THE CYNICS will always argue that cricket isn't what it used to be. Neither is photography or the visual representation of cricket. It is now possible to sit in an armchair almost anywhere in the world and watch live cricket, relayed by satellite. We have become more efficient, more comprehensive in the way we cover sport, and more frantic in our consumption of this coverage. In cricketing terms, the last thirty years have seen the death of the distinctions between Gentleman and Player, the birth of the one-day international and the four-day county match, and the death of the three-day game. The World Cup has arrived. Cricketers wear the logos of their backers, use a white ball, and are subject to greater pressures than The Doctor, The Master or The Don could ever have conceived.

To some, all this is a disaster, a rapid slide into an unhappy land of snarling headlines, lager-soaked crowds, helmetted heroes, slow over rates, slog and gallop games, the reverse sweep, and disrespect for the custodians and spirit of cricket. To others, cricket has been saved from a slower slide into oblivion, thanks to large injections of cash and to the exploits of Imran Khan, Kapil Dev, Richard Hadlee, Malcolm Marshall, Viv Richards and Ian Botham. In a couple of seasons in the early 1980s, Botham almost single-handedly put English cricket back on the front page of newspapers.

Cricket photography has kept pace with all this. The demands placed on a contemporary cricket photographer may best be illustrated by a case study. In *Sports Photography* (1984), Steve Powell and Tony Duffy describe the workload of Adrian Murrell when he covered the 1976-77 England tour of India. He had five separate clients. The *Daily Express* wanted a regular supply of 'pictures of the day' from the five Test matches. Hodder and Stoughton wanted fifty pictures covering the tour for Scyld Berry's book, *Cricket Wallah*. The *Observer* wanted Murrell to wire back to England shots of any

Worcestershire v
Gloucestershire, Gillette
Cup Semi-Final,
Worcester, 1973.
R.G.A. Headley loses
his bat to a high-bouncing
ball from D.A.
Graveney. Sports Picture
of the Year, 1973.
Photograph: Ken Kelly.

England v West Indies,
second Test, Edgbaston,
1973. G. St.A. (Sir
Garfield) Sobers driving.
The wicketkeeper is
A.P.E. Knott.
Photograph: Patrick Eagar

Saturday action for use in Sunday's edition. *The Cricketer* wanted thirty or forty good black-and-white pictures every week. Finally, Murrell had to send regular colour photographs back to his own All-Sport Library.

Much of this would be impossible without modern technology. Not only can the contemporary cricket photographer take more pictures more easily (thanks to improvements in lenses and film, and to such innovations as the motor drive camera), but also the speed with which they can be reproduced, and the quality of the reproductions obtained, have left

much of the past far behind. A little over 100 years ago we were almost starved of cricket photographs; now there is a glut. The end of the agency monopoly made it possible for anyone to photograph top-class cricket. This is not to suggest that life is easy for the modern cricket photographer. Equipment is still heavy enough to make moving around a cricket ground only marginally easier than moving around the Crimea was for Roger Fenton. And it is not unknown for players and officials to make life difficult.

In an age when it appears all too easy to obtain fine action pictures of the highlights of a day's play, some picture editors have preferred the dramatic shot which illustrates the less happy aspects of the game. The picture of Keith Fletcher hitting the stumps in frustration at being given out in India in 1981 was printed in the *Daily Express*. According to Powell and Duffy, publishing this picture 'was a major contributing factor in Fletcher losing the England captaincy'. Chris Broad's career was certainly not helped by pictures of his frustration when dismissed in more than one Test match. Considerable prominence has also been given to photographs of rows between Javed Miandad and Dennis Lillee, Mike Gatting and Umpire Shakoor Rana, and Fletcher and Umpires Krishan and Ramaswami.

The prying eye has the ability to show us good and ill, to act as counsel for the prosecution and the defence, to justify or to condemn. Photography has provided solid evidence of the illegal action of Meckiff, Griffin and, from time to time, Lock. There are pictures that speak eloquently of the physical battering given Brian Close and John Edrich by the West Indian fast bowlers at Old Trafford in 1976. The camera has also, however, shown that Mike Procter did not bowl off the wrong foot, as many had thought, and has vindicated as many umpires as it has proved mistaken. At a decisive moment in the Edgbaston Test in 1985, the sequence of photographs taken by Ken Kelly of Gower's catch off Lamb's instep to dismiss Allan Border proved that the catch was good, despite Australian objections. Whether any of all of this shows too much intrusion into the game is a matter for debate. Perhaps in the long run, it is simply a question of what we find most memorable in cricket – temperament or temper, a century or a sensation. Sometimes, the relationship between the cricket photographer and his subject has its

good-humoured side, as when Bradman obligingly slowed down his walk to the wicket at Headingley in 1948 to allow Ken Kelly, Jack Hickes and Jack Fletcher time to take the photographs of him that they needed.

In some ways, the famous cricketer has always been a celebrity, fair game for informal pictures of moments of relaxation. We have already seen how Grace and Bradman were

Bishan Bedi. The photographer took four years to capture the precise angle of Bedi's hands just before the moment of delivery, and would have been prepared to wait twenty years. Photograph: Ken Kelly

photographed wherever they went. Ninety years ago Trumper was in the limelight – one newspaper even published a picture of him playing the piano in his London hotel while Clem Hill looked on approvingly. Warwick Armstrong's powerful side of 1921 attracted much attention as they swept from victory to victory. All this was with the full consent of the players involved, but the skill (or perhaps the cunning) of the modern photographer takes us further. There is no dressing-room privacy anywhere near the windows these days. The honest cricket photographer is not looking for trouble, nor seeking to make the professional lives of cricketers uncomfortable, but much can be read into an off-guard picture of a dispirited captain as his side goes down, or a disgruntled batsman on his return to the pavilion.

Cricket photography has always had a place for the novelty picture – Sewell in gas mark, or Grace resting his head on J.R. Mason's shoulders. Recent times have seen an increase in such pictures. The bomb scare at Lord's in 1973 produced a series of memorable photographs, including Patrick Eagar's shot of police pleading with a stubborn member to leave his place in the stand, and Ken Kelly's picture of Umpire Dicky Bird perched on the wicket covers. One of the most dramatic cricket photographs of a break in play was that taken by a Sport & General cameraman at Lord's during the Second World War. A

German flying bomb flew over and the players threw themselves on the ground. In the tradition of Lionel Tennyson and Len Hutton batting one-handed, recent times have produced pictures of Malcolm Marshall, with a double-fracture of his left thumb, batting against England at Headingley in July 1984, and of Paul Terry, with a broken arm, fending off the West Indies at Old Trafford a fortnight later. One of the most popular cricket novelty pictures is that of Derek Randall turning a celebratory cartwheel when England beat Australia at Headingley in 1977 – the camera missed it first time round, and Randall generously obliged by turning a second cartwheel to order.

Modern times have also seen, for many, the demise of the group picture. Looking back at the photographs of touring and international sides 130 years ago, we see teams as we suspect they always were – clusters of individuals, disparate collections of sportsmen gathered together for an afternoon, a weekend, or for several months, simply to play cricket. And, on any particular day, they sat down or stood around together for a few minutes, and were photographed. The camera has caught something that was there already. There is a lovely picture of the 1913-14 MCC touring team to South Africa, taken in the street. There is no sense of uniformity. Some wear bow ties, some wear club ties, Tennyson wears

Kent v Hampshire, Basingstoke, 1974. M.C. Cowdrey is hit by a rising ball from A.M.E. Roberts. Cowdrey took no further part in the match. The sequence was taken using a 16mm Bolex cine camera, adapted for stills use, at approximately sixty frames per second. Photographs: Patrick Eagar

Australia v Pakistan, first Test, Perth, November 1981. A.R. Crafter (umpire) intervenes in a confrontation between D.K. Lillee and Javed Miandad.
Source: West Australian Newspapers Ltd.

England v India, 1982.
Y. Sharma, S.M.H.
Kirmani and D.I.
Gower collide.
Photograph: Patrick
Eagar

no tie at all. There are round collars and pointed collars. Rhodes sports a flat cap, Douglas holds a boater. We can tell the gentlemen from the players, the happy-go-lucky adventurers from the earnest professionals. Sadly, today, all of this appears to have gone. A team picture now is an exercise in discipline and uniformity. Those standing at the back must all have their hands behind their backs. Those seated must all have their hands resting on their knees. Whites and blazers will be worn: the sponsor's logo will be prominently displayed at all times. The photographer is not asked to take a picture of something that is there, but to create something out of an ad-man's imagination. This is not to say that the surpassing cricket photograph has disappeared – far from it. There are as many wonderful cricket pictures being taken today as there ever were.

The cricket photograph has also achieved the ultimate in respectability. All over the world, collectors bid for pictures, flickers,

lantern slides, photogravures, postcards, cigarette cards, programmes and brochures, badges and calendars of cricket. In the 1980s prices began to rise sharply at sales and auctions. A single picture can fetch as much as £1200. Treasure troves are still being rescued from their cobwebbed sleep, in attics and cellars, in old trunks and chests, and in the offices of local newspapers. Recognition has been given, albeit belatedly, to the artistry as well as the craftsmanship of the cricket photographer. Proper steps are being taken to restore old pictures and to preserve them. The *Wisden Cricket Monthly* for January 1987 published an account of the 'retrieval' of a photograph taken by H.A. 'Ozzie' Osborne in 1892 of the game between England and Australia at the Sydney Cricket Ground. The picture is thought by many to be the earliest known of a Test in Australia.

Perhaps the most obvious development in recent times has been the profusion of colour pictures of cricket. A hundred or more years

England v Australia, Edgbaston, 1985. W.B. Phillips is caught by D.I. Gower off the boot of A.J. Lamb. The Australians doubted that the catch was good. These three photographs show that it was. Photograph: Ken Kelly

ago, the public had to be content with hand-coloured photographs and *cartes-de-visite*. Early stages of colour photography were largely confined to the cinematograph industry. In 1905 Pathecolor was introduced – a print of the film to be coloured was projected one frame at a time on to a small screen and the operator outlined all the areas in the frame to be tinted a particular colour. In 1911 Kinemacolor and Biocolor appeared, the latter being simply the staining of alternate frames on the film red and green. A year later came the Gaumont Chronochrome process, whereby the camera had three lenses – one with a red filter, one with green, and one with blue – and the colour was directly photographed on to the film. Technicolor and Kodachrome both started in 1922, though three-colour technicolor didn't appear until ten years later. Little exists of early colour pictures of cricket as there was such a small latitude for cameras to

England v Australia, Old Trafford, 1985. H.D. Bird (umpire) has had enough and draws stumps. Photograph: Patrick Eagar

England v Australia,
Headingley, 1985.
I.T. Botham gives
G.F. Lawson a bouncer.
Photograph: Adrian
Murrell/All-Sport

New Zealand v England,
Christchurch, 1988.
J.E.Emburey and
C.W.J. Athey drop R.J.
(Sir Richard) Hadlee.
Photograph: Graham
Morris

give the correct exposure. The cricket photographer had enough difficulty capturing the important moments of the game without having constantly to check any slight changes in the light or the angle of the sun. There are colour pictures of Bradman in the nets taken before the Second World War, and more general colour coverage of cricket from the 1950s onwards.

The big increase in colour photography of cricket, however, took place in the early 1970s. Technical improvements led to better cameras and to colour film with a much faster speed, and with this came an increasing demand for colour pictures. For some, the colour cricket photograph is at its best in general views of grounds or in cricket landscapes, but colour detracts from most action shots. The problem is that colour background can often dominate what should be the centrepiece of the picture. Green is far more obtrusive than grey, and, with ground level shots, where a section of the crowd often forms the background, there may well be vivid splashes of colour that draw the

England v West Indies, Lord's 1988. M.D. Marshall and R.B. Richardson celebrate the dismissal of another English batsman. Photograph: Patrick Eagar

eye irritatingly away from the action, from the reason for the photograph. On the other hand, few would be prepared to do without colour entirely, but it is mainly the extreme close-up shot that gains from colour – such as the wonderful sequence of pictures of Michael Holding taken by Patrick Eagar at the Oval Test in 1976, when 'the whispering death' took 14 for 149 on what John Woodcock of *The Times* described as 'one of the world's deadest pitches'. There is Holding, the sweat bursting from him, dust rising beneath his feet, his arm swinging straight and fast in his follow-through, with the ball already in flight. If only such technical sophistication had existed in the days of Richardson, Lohmann, Jones, Kotze or Kortright...

One final point: the cricket photograph has come a long way since Fenton's early study, the faint and faded portraits of 'Silver Billy' Beldham and others, and the pictures of those cricketers who sailed to the United States while Dickens was still struggling with *A Tale of Two Cities*. We are immeasurably fortunate in the thousands of photographs that we have of the last 130 years of the game. We know how Grace stood, how Lord Harris dressed for cricket, how Hobbs moved to the ball, how Tate grasped the ball, how Jardine looked when he took the field, how Bradman cut and Hammond drove, how Trueman flung his

body forward as he hurled the ball down and how Laker's left wrist bent back at the moment of delivery. We can relive the catches of Miller and Surridge, Simpson and Cowdrey, even see how Jessop and Constantine swooped to pick up the ball. As for the heroes of the past, so for those of the present and future – we shall never be without pictures of great players and great cricket. But the novelty of photography has worn off. Among these thousands of cricket pictures, some that are most to be treasured are those of crowds and queues; of little boys

The touring Australian team at a press conference on arrival in the UK in April 1989.
Photograph: Patrick Eagar

asking for autographs; of mighty rollers and the men and horses that pulled them; of the game played on beach and bombsite, brickfield and back-alley, village green and city square. Are we still capturing the flavour of all that surrounds and envelops cricket? A cricket photograph of 1890 records a scene and a world so very different from one of 1860. Have we allowed the camera to catch the same generation of difference between 1990 and 1960? Perhaps we are putting too much pressure on photographers to get the pictures we think we must have, and not allowing them enough time for the pictures they would like to take, and for the pictures that will mean so much in another 130 years' time.

CHAPTER 8

The View
from Behind
the Lens

*'You don't get to see what's going on. You stand round at the end of
the day with your mates, and they say "what a great day's cricket!"
I haven't a clue. One day I would like to take a
Test off and go and sit and watch it.'*
– Graham Morris, cricket photographer

THE MOMENT a photograph is taken, it becomes an historical document, an *aide memoire*, a small and possibly misleading piece of evidence. Taken as a whole, cricket photographs provide us with the only means we have of seeing the heroes who performed in front of our ancestors.

Contemporary professional cricket photographers are conscious of the weight of archive material that exists, and conscious that they are adding to it. Every photographer has his collection of pictures; some have their own archives. The difference is that archives are no longer created by bringing together as many existing pictures as possible. Archives are created to the specifications of present-day picture editors, designers and commissioning editors. If the *Observer* or the *Sunday Times,* the *Guardian* or the *Independent* wants a horizontal picture that will spread across five columns, then that is what will be taken. Few photographers are in the happy position of seeking only to please themselves. In 100 years

time, we shall discover that cricket in the 1990s was extensively and wonderfully covered by the camera, but within limits. Almost every slip catch taken in a Lord's Test will be there, with every streaker, bomb scare, disputed decision and cartwheeling stump.

Perhaps this is being too pessimistic: it is certainly doing less than justice to the perspiring cameraman. A day in the life of a professional cricket photographer is long and arduous. 'Cricket,' says Graham Morris, 'has got to be one of the most boring things in the world to photograph.' All agree that it is physically hard work. Lugging cameras, lenses, tripods, rolls of film (each photographer may shoot twenty or more rolls of 35mm film in a day), spare batteries and sandwiches needs sustained energy. All agree that the level of concentration is exhausting, even though a day's work may eventually last only 1/125th of a seond. Patrick Eagar may have three or more cameras in place, one of which may be on the opposite side of the ground, worked by remote

Australia v West Indies,
World Series Cup Final,
Melbourne, 1985.
J. Dujon takes off.
Photograph: Adrian
Murrell/All-Sport

control. To know which camera to fire, from which angle, with which type of film, and in which order needs great concentration. The photographer also has to keep some kind of record of what pictures have been taken. In 1956 Central Press lost their monopoly at Old Trafford to Sport & General for one Test, which happened to be the one in which Jim Laker took nineteen wickets. As they used up plate after plate, Ken Saunders and Brian Thomas had to make sure they knew which picture was which. It was not an easy job, for all Laker's wickets were taken from the Stretford End: five were caught by Oakman; two by Cowdrey and two by Lock; Craig was lbw to Laker in both Australian innings; and Mackay was caught Oakman bowled Laker for 0 twice.

The cricket photographer's day is a long one. Adrian Murrell would expect to arrive at Lord's at 8 am on the morning of a Test, unload his equipment, set up his cameras and get into position. From then on, until 6 pm, he would watch every ball. 'It's a business,' he says. 'You can't just wander off and have a sandwich. You look at it brutally – what am I trying to achieve? Who am I taking this picture for?' Patrick Eagar has the same sense of being tied to the cricket: 'The essence of the game happens in an instant, you get no warning. You daren't miss a ball, so any maintenance has to be done during lunch or tea. And maintenance can be anything from changing a film, having a pee, making an appointment with somebody, having a cold drink if it's a hot day, or, if it's a cold day, warming up somehow. I'd say it was non stop until seven...you don't have time to talk to people. Occasionally you're in a sheer panic – you don't realise you've run out of film in a camera.'

The variables in cricket – at once the terror and delight to all of us – are constant in one way only: they make life harder for the photographer. As the light worsens during a traditional English summer day, the photographer has to keep changing the film in his or her cameras, always using the film with the slowest possible speed. The photographer is reluctant to switch to a higher-speed film, knowing that this always means a loss of quality. We are no longer amazed and excited simply at seeing a photograph of a dramatic stumping or run out. The photograph has also to be of the finest quality and definition – the picture editor, acting on our behalf, takes this for granted.

Towards the end of a season, some cricketers begin to suffer from camera fatigue. Dennis Oulds tells the story of when he was taking a picture of the Yorkshire team back in the 1960s. Trueman protested: 'What! Another ★★★★★★ group! Haven't you taken enough of us lot?' Oulds replied: 'Think of the time when you won't be sitting there, Fred.' Trueman saw his point. 'Aye,' he said. 'You're reet, Dennis. Make it a good 'un.' It took all Oulds's powers of persuasion to convince Len Hutton that he should find time for a photograph of the England team that regained the Ashes at the Oval in 1953. On the last morning, with England needing only fifty runs for victory, Hutton was still opposed to the idea, but, with only a quarter-of-an-hour left before start of play, Oulds played his ace: 'Do you realise,' he said, 'that you won't have a picture of yourself as captain of England on this historic occasion? What will your grandchildren say?' The picture, signed by all the team, appeared in every paper the following morning.

Even when a team does agree to being photographed (or when a team has been persuaded by its sponsor to co-operate with a photographer), success is not guaranteed. In the Bicentenary Test at Lords in 1987, Eagar decided to take pictures (with a plate camera) of not only the MCC side and the Rest of the World side, but one enormous photograph of cricketers old and new, 180 people in all. It was not easy to get all 180 to look at him at the same time: Eagar feels that a Victorian photographer would have made a better job of that, or that he should have had a whistle, for disciplinary purposes. Once the picture had been taken, however, Eagar wanted to take greater care than usual over its processing. Quality which is adequate for reproduction in a newspaper or a

Centenary Test, Lord's 1980. This photograph of all available English and Australian players lined up on the morning of the second day was taken on a 4x5 inch plate camera.

Photograph: Patrick Eagar

magazine, is not good enough for museum records or for display in a photographic gallery or on a pavilion wall. When Eagar took large group pictures at the Centenary Tests at Melbourne in 1977 and at Lord's in 1980, he felt that he had in some ways compromised by using a 35mm camera in Melbourne and a 5 x 4 camera in London. Some of the late Victorian photographs (those in the pavilion at the Oval, for example), which Eagar greatly admires, were taken on 15 x 12 plates, slightly enlarged, and almost certainly specially toned with gold or platinum toner. For the Centenary Test photograph, Eagar persuaded

Kodak to print four copies of the picture to archival standards, to give it a life of at least 100 years. No one in Britain knew how this was to be done, and help had to be called in from Rochester, New York. There are now four such copies of the picture – two at Lord's (one for the MCC and one for the TCCB), one in Melbourne, and one in the care of Eagar himself.

Modern cricket photography is an expensive business. When an England team goes abroad, national newspapers cannot afford to send staff or contract photographers with them. A freelance photographer has to take the chance that he or she will sell enough pictures (to

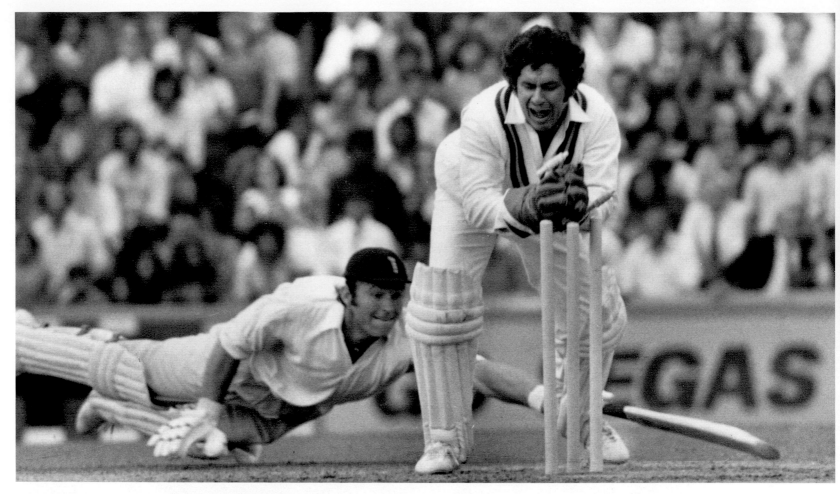

*England v Pakistan, the
Oval, 1974. Wasim Bari
fails to stump D.L. Amiss
in the opinion of the
umpire, succeeds in the
opinion of the camera.
Photograph: Ken Kelly*

papers, magazines, brochures, souvenir journals, and so on) to cover the costs of living and working abroad for maybe four or five months. For the 1992 World Cup, All-Sport sent three photographers and two technicians to Australia and New Zealand. Two of the photographers followed the progress of the England team – one to take ground level pictures (which Adrian Murrell considers the most powerful and effective) and one to take shots from above the action (to ensure a featureless background).

Developments in photographic technology have made it possible to send high-quality colour pictures by telephone in a matter of minutes from any part of the world, but, to meet the demands of the market, the contemporary photographer may be as cluttered by impedimenta as Roger Fenton was 135 years ago. All-Sport now have a large van, maybe twice the size of Fenton's Photographic Carriage, equipped both to process and transmit pictures from any location in the world. The vehicle has a mini processing

laboratory, built-in telephones that can be linked to land lines, and cellular telephones for transmission by satellite. It's a far cry from the days when Murrell and Eagar had to make friends with the staff of local papers in Calcutta or Lahore, and then queue at the local Post Office to wire their pictures back to London.

So much changes, so much stays the same. Dennis Oulds of Central Press and Ken Saunders of Sport & General used to send their pictures to three London evening papers (*Star, Evening News* and *Evening Standard*), as well as sixty or seventy other newspapers. On a national scale, the turnaround was fast. 'When covering cricket at the Oval,' recalls Oulds, 'a photograph could be delievered to a newspaper twenty-five minutes after it had been taken. Dispatch riders using Norton HRD motorbikes collected the negatives from the Oval and delivered them to the Central Press offices. Wet processing and printing was used, and the same messengers then delievered the prints to newspapers. Problems arose with slow cricket.

You could watch Len Hutton for three-quarters of an hour before anything happened.' Nowadays, faced with such a problem, a photographer might well move to some other part of the ground, to seek a fresh angle. For Oulds and Saunders there was no such luxury. The Oval had three photographic positions: the roof of the Vauxhall Stand, the Pavilion (looking down the wicket – something of a luxury), and the Secretary's Office or the balcony of the Committee Room. For Saunders at Lord's there were greater restrictions. The MCC may have wanted every match to be photographed, but they did little to facilitate the photographer's task. The three positions at Lord's were on Q stand (next to the pavilion – where Saunders used a 48-inch Long Tom marked in focusing ranges of 2, 3, 4, 5, 7, 10, 15 yards and infinity), on the flat roof of the old Tavern (side on to the wicket), and on a bridge between Q stand and the pavilion (a position from which both wickets could be covered by a 28-inch lens).

Then, as now, it helped if the cameraman was able to build up a happy working relationship with cricketers. Dennis Oulds had reason to be grateful to Bradman in 1948 for re-staging a presentation which he had failed to capture. Adrian Murrell, on twelve England tours, has had the opportunity to become friendly with many England players. Ideally, there is a sense of trust between player and photographer. In return for making themselves available for pictures, players receive free prints and pictures for their benefit brochures or other souvenirs. They also have the comfort of knowing that they won't suffer the photographic fate of, say, the Royal Family in having their every unguarded moment immortalised. Anything that happens out in the middle may be fair game for a picture, but most photographers are aware that there are other occasions when a photograph, surreptitiously taken, could do harm to a cricketer. There is also the problem of what use is made of a legitimately taken photograph. A picture of a cricketer yawning on the field may be cruelly captioned by a waspish sub-editor.

It also helps if a photographer knows his cricket, as George Beldam did in the old days. Adrian Murrell explains that a cricket photographer has to try to read the game. 'You look for any friction between players – for example [in 1992] Gower and Gooch looking at each other quizzically…your lens is your ear. You can hear everything through your lens.' In the words of Patrick Eagar: 'You're constantly betting. You're saying "I think the most likely thing to happen at the moment is that there's going to be a catch in this area, or, conversely, well, these two are dead set…let's forget about them being out and get some batting pictures from them." And then something goes against the run of play…The thing about photography is that you're trained to make instant reactions based on visual clues, and often you've taken the good photograph before you quite realise what you've done. I don't think any of us sit down and say "Ah! I think these two policeman are going to symbolise the steadiness of the situation and Hobbs and Sutcliffe are going to symbolise England." But you might say "Well, a symmetrical composition's often quite a good thing, and if I can get the two policeman here rather than there that might make a more interesting photograph".' More prosaically, Eagar adds that the picture in question was most probably taken to provide something from the first hour's play, when the only likely alternatives might simply have been Hobbs or Sutcliffe playing defensively.

Which brings us to the problem of The One That Got Away. Every photographer has his or her sad story to tell. For Graham Morris, it is of the disappearing negative – a picture he took at Sharjah when England played Australia. Greg Matthews bowled to Tim Robinson. The ball shot up in front of the batsman, who slumped down on his knees. Steve Rixon, the Australian wicketkeeper, sensing that Robinson had hit the ball, dived over the stumps and over Robinson's crouching figure, to catch the ball in front of the batsman. For Adrian Murrell, it is of a flash fault. He was in the Australian dressing room in Sydney when Australia won

England v West Indies, the Oval, 1984. Two views of the same event by the same photographer showing the difference in effect resulting from two completely different viewpoints. H.A. Gomes caught I.T. Botham bowled R.M. Ellison. Photographs: Patrick Eagar

England tour of West Indies, 1990. View of Warner Park, St Kitts. Photograph: Patrick Eagar

G.R.J. Matthews makes his catch despite helping seagulls. Photograph: Graham Morris

England v Australia,
Texaco Trophy, Lord's,
1989. Photographers at
work beneath the Tavern
scoreboard.
Photograph: Patrick Eagar

the Ashes. He shot a whole film of the celebrations. Not one picture came out. He was unable to speak, civilly, to anyone for twenty-four hours. For Dennis Oulds, it is a matter of the sheer bulk of a 48-inch lens. 'A great picture we all missed was during a Test match at Old Trafford. Lindsay Hassett was fielding on the boundary and missed a sitter of a catch. He eased his embarrassment by strolling to a policeman sitting on a box at the edge of the crowd, and removing the policeman's helmet. Hassett then stood, holding the helmet in a catching position, to a roar of approval from the crowd. Meanwhile, we were all frantically swinging our cameras on to the incident – a forlorn hope, as Hassett replaced the policeman's helmet and continued patrolling the boundary long before we were able to get there. The groans of photographers must have been heard in the city.'

Oulds suffered a near miss with one of the most famous cricket photographs of all time,

Underwood taking the last Australian wicket at the Oval in 1968. 'At lunchtime a tropical storm broke over the Oval and in a few moments the playing area was under water... Dozens of spectators were asked to prod sticks into the area to help clear the water. By three o'clock the outfield was like a mud heap but the water had disappeared. Around four-thirty Cowdrey and the umpires came out. "You've run out of time, Colin," I said. "Give me an hour-and-a-half and we'll see," he replied. Unbelievably, play started around five o'clock – the match had to end at six-thirty. After a couple of overs from the fast men, Cowdrey brought 'Deadly' Derek Underwood into the attack on a wicket made for him. He was completely unplayable. Eventually the whole side were within a few paces of the batsmen...An idiot could have taken good pictures – it was just a question of waiting for catches. The Aussies were hypnotised by Underwood and he got the

last wicket with time to spare. They were unique pictures. I had never seen a fielding side so close, with everyone on camera and David Brown fielding at the end of the bat.' But the Fleet Street blockmakers were on strike, and not a single London paper carried the picture the next day.

I write this on the second day of the Lord's Test in June 1992. Every daily paper carries pictures of the previous day's play, mainly of Waqar Younis's triumphs as he took 5 for 91.

The *Daily Mirror* has one photograph; the *Sun* has two; the *Daily Star* has three; the *Daily Express* and the *Daily Mail* have two; the *Independent*, the *Guardian* and the *Daily Telegraph* have one; and the *Times* has two. In addition, there will be dozens in magazines, souvenir journals, books and brochures.

A hundred years ago it was a different story, one without pictures – and, as Alice thought, 'What is the use of a book without pictures?'

England v West Indies, fifth Test, 1986. R.A. Harper leaps to exchange a high five with I.V.A. Richards after bowling I.T. Botham. Photograph: Gordon Brooks

155

England v Australia, Centenary Test, Lord's 1980. Dennis Oulds with almost the last of the Long Toms.
Photograph: Patrick Eagar

RIGHT: *India v South Africa, Nehru Stadium, Delhi, 1991. View of spectators.*
Photograph: David Munden

Patrick Eagar, taken by
Adrian Murrell, 1987.

LEFT: *Sydney Cricket*
Ground, World Cup,
1992.
Photograph: David
Munden

Index